MW01709655

# One 11 Millionth of a War

★ ★ ★


Lt. Colonel Frank Maleckas, Jr., retired
307th Bomb Group
13th Air Force


Ever in peace rejoice

Frank Maleckas

*On the front cover:*
*A "Long Ranger" of the 307th Bomber Group moments after flak hit over Manila, January 31, 1945.*
*Navigator Frank Maleckas, Jr., at right, with bomber co-pilot Masters, at left, and bombadier Sedor taken in 1942.*

Library of Congress CIP 00-108755



ISBN 0-9742686-0-7

Book production by Bookability, Inc.
P.O. Box 843, Elk Rapids, MI 49629
(231) 264-5851

# Ever in peace may every land rejoice

*- Thomas Carlyle Adamson*

It is only with the editing, typing, and footwork of my son, Aldon, and the urging and encouragement of Helen, my wife, and Janet, my daughter, that this story is published.

# Prologue

The army is so big and it's a wonder that more men don't get lost in it. Every once in a while a story comes our way of men who did get lost. A particularly pathetic note was struck by the plight of a solitary aviator on a far-off island in the Solomons. Before his plane crashed in the sea, he bailed out. He made a successful water landing and swam through miles of churning seas to drop exhausted on a stony island beach.

There, friendly natives found him. They fed him, housed him, and cared for all his needs. An even greater piece of luck seemed to befall him. In the neighborhood was a coast watcher employed as a sort of spy and messenger by all colonial interests. He carried the news of the flier's whereabouts back to Army and Navy authorities. In due course, his outfit was informed of the situation. Then, months passed without further word. In the evening at the club, the boys would speculate from time to time. It was generally assumed that the Navy had picked him up. His buddies envied him as they pictured him somewhere back in the States.

The Navy, meanwhile, had been engaged otherwise, what with the war and one thing after another. The man was pigeonholed. Then, one-day word came into Navy headquarters that natives had captured a Japanese soldier and taken him to that island. Instantly, a party set out to pick up and question that Japanese soldier. They had transacted their business with the natives and were preparing to leave with the prisoner when a strange bearded man came out of the jungle. He looked well but unhappy.

The sailors looked at him questioningly. His skin was brown as a Polynesian's, but his eyes were blue. He spoke in a forlorn but strangely Brooklyn-esque accent, "Bud," he said, "can I get a lift out of here."

*- From an Army newspaper, 1943 or 1944*

# Forward

The United States' Army, during World War II, had about eleven million troops by the time hostilities ceased. One may think of it as a vast body of eleven million units engaged in a colossal undertaking with each unit supplying one 11 millionth of the total energy. Each could not contribute more than all it had to give

Trumpets heralded the end of the great drive. Victory at last! Members of the great Army could each proudly proclaim that they had each supplied one full 11 millionth of the total effort towards that victory.

*My first bomber crew. Front row (kneeling left to right): Dzingoski, McNabb, Hall. Back row (standing left to right): Carter, Riley, Peters, Maleckas (me), Sedor, Masters, and Aldon A. Alleman, our pilot. I do not remember all of their first names.*

## In Memory of Aldon A. Alleman's Crew

*They answered the call*
*To counter the scourge*
*They gave full measure*
*And now they rest*
*In a quiet place*
*And made a more tranquil world.*

# Introduction

Over 11 million people served in the armies of the United States during World War II. Each one of them has a unique story to tell. All would range from somewhat comic, to painfully moving, to supremely tragic. Unfortunately, most of the stories will never be told. What can be learned from the sacrifices will not be known.

A phenomenon common among the participants in this war is that those who were most heavily engaged are least inclined to talk about it, except, perhaps among themselves. I served over four years and represent about one 11-millionth of the army's war effort. I have talked of my experiences to few groups that were genuinely interested. Often people would suggest and sometimes urge that I write about them. Though no two experiences are alike, I always felt that my trials, though severe, were all together too common.

As years passed and I reflected on what I did on behalf of individual liberty, I began to feel good about what I contributed. Also, I came to know some fine people who felt that a written account would be of much interest. So, I am making an effort to write and make a record of one 11-millionth of a war effort as seen through the eyes of one heavy bomber navigator. After 40 years it will be necessary to tug hard on the memory. Details will be frayed and there will be need to interpolate and extrapolate. For example, if "A" happened and "C" happened, then "B" must have happened. In this way the drama will come to life.

I was a part of four crews. Aldon A. Alleman piloted the first crew. This crew was lost on January 5, 1943 while flying in Kansas. I was the lone survivor. After the crash, I went back to Tucson to pick up a new crew. Robert W. Daniels piloted this crew. I trained with this crew about a month or so. Daniels became ill. I was ordered to fly with a temporary crew. They were flying reconnaissance into the central Pacific. After eight missions, I came back to Tucson. Daniels had been assigned another navigator. This crew eventually went to Italy and was lost. I do not know if there were any survivors. I was a loose navigator for a few days. Then, I received an urgent order to fly to Hamilton Field, California. I was assigned to Gene B. Snyder's crew whose navigator became disqualified. Some said he had lost his nerve. As a member of Gene's crew, I flew into the south Pacific combat area. Gene broke down in New Zealand. I was then assigned to Kenneth Greear's crew. His navigator had been wounded. This crew was lost. I was the lone survivor. After recovering from my ordeal, I learned that Gene Snyder had recovered. He and his crew eventually were shot down over Rabaul. There were no survivors.

*We took the stance to thwart the foe*
*From those who fell we took the torch*
*And held it high to keep the faith*
*We bid them rest in quiet peace*
*While great engines hummed*
*We sought to secure a tranquil world.*

*My fourth bomber crew. Their last flight October 25, 1943. Front row, left to right: F. Kniest, C. Godsey, P. Kish, K. Greear. Rear row, left to right: C. Gentry, E. Stone, J. Murphy, C. Shannon, M. Sech, E. Cooler. C. Godsey survived. He was wounded in previous raid. I took his place.*

# Chapter 1

In the first week of February 1943, the whole of our heavy bombardment training group moved from Alamogordo Army Air Base to Bliss Field at El Paso, Texas. Something mysterious was being constructed to the north of Alamogordo, so we had to abandon the bombing range and field facilities and move south. We wondered about the big construction project near the bombing targets. We could only speculate over the project and soon forgot about it.

Training in heavy bombers was divided into three phases of one month each. At Bliss field we settled down into the second phase of training. For me it was a second time through these phases.

The first phase in the B24's was done at Tucson Army Air Base where emphasis was on making the pilot proficient in handling the airplane. Also, the crew was assembled and taught to work as a team.

The second phase was completed in Alamogordo, New Mexico. Most of this flying time was spent practicing precision bombing. Normally, we took up 20 to 100 practice bombs and dropped them one at a time on a desert bull's eye. They made a big flash and a puff-of-smoke, but little else. The hit was recorded by ground observers and went on the bombardier's record, as well as the crew's. It took practiced coordination between pilot and bombardier to make a successful hit. With a number of other bombers taking turns, it took hours to make 20 passes over the target.

Toward the end of the second phase, some navigation flights were made involving a flight to some distant point, either straight in or with several course changes en route. This didn't occur often enough for me, but we were in a hurry to produce ready crews.

The third phase of the training was completed at some northern base where crews were involved in cold weather and bad weather flying. Upon completion, we were declared combat ready as far as training in the U.S. was concerned. Still more advanced skills were to be learned in the particular combat zones.

As we settled down into our second phase at Bliss Field, I recalled my first three phases of training. We had begun training in October 1942. We were declared combat ready in Topeka, Kansas, at the end of December 1942.

We had become a very close group of men much attached to each other, and looked after each other against the hazards downtown. Often we talked about how we would come to each other's aid in various emergencies. We conjured some weird ones.

In particular, the waist gunner often said to me, "Lieutenant, I'm going to see to it that you take no dangerous chances with the women when we go to town." This he did well, but it was an easy task for him for I was a shy guy and not much inclined toward ventures. Neither of us normally drank, but in these times we partook of the spirits that in quiet time we would have passed up. Topeka was a "dry" city and Kansas was a "dry" state. Still, we observed more drunk troops here than in the "wet" states in which we trained.

Our pilot was from California. He was a mild fellow, very able in his job and quiet spoken. After three months of training, we could execute his commands while he was still thinking about them. The copilot was from Kentucky. He and the pilot were one.

The bombardier hailed from Chicago and was a big man. His "circular error" was among the best. Still, we all teased him about how bad it was. We said his good record was all a mistake that must be investigated. He, also, was a top musician who had made tours throughout Europe.

The radio operator came from Louisiana and was a waist gunner.

The flight engineer was a Michigan boy, older than most of us. He had worked in the oil fields before the army. He operated the top turret.

The tail turret man came from Texas. The front turret man was from New Mexico.

The ball gunner came from New York and had the meanest job on the crew. He did his fighting rolled up like a ball with his knees by his shoulders.

The second waist gunner was from Brooklyn. He loved to look after people and did. He made this request of me, "Lieutenant, if I get my genitals shot off, promise that you'll shoot me in the head." It was difficult for me to wiggle out of that one and never did completely.

All through December we familiarized ourselves with all the nastiness that cold weather, snow, and storms could throw at the rugged B24 airplane and us. Of particular discomfort were the 40 to 60 degree below zero temperatures at high altitude. It was difficult to remove ice formed on various parts of the plane. No matter how heavily clothed we were, it was never enough to keep us in any sort of comfort. Shivering was the only way we could warm up enough to survive. There was also a limit to the amount of clothing we could put on. More clothes meant more bulk and more bulk made us immobile in the plane. The bomber, big as it was, was very limited on inside space. The designers seemed to have forgotten that bulky men must move inside it. They filled it with every sort of apparatus. Men were to accommodate themselves the best they could. Thus, we were to go to war.

At the end of our third phase in Topeka, there was a few days lull while the generals pondered high strategy and great battles while we brave ones waited. We all knew that before long we would have to charge. While waiting, we spent some evenings in Topeka engaged in mindless diversions that would shut out the future.

The pilot stayed behind most of the time writing letters home and laying groundwork for a business he was planning. He had a fantastic and revolutionary idea about a design for helicopters. He was determined to manufacture them as soon as he left the Army. When time allowed, he was thinking, planning, and lining up people.

I was to be one of the important cogs in this enterprise. He needed a mathematician. I was to fill this position. Math was my college major and I agreed realizing that a serious undertaking such as building advanced state-of-the-art helicopters would be a taxing job. I determined to succeed, and began to edge toward advanced mathematics. The design he had in mind was a closed secret with him. He allowed me to see bits and pieces. The world had a great helicopter coming.

On excursions into town, the bombardier, copilot, and I went together. The pilot simply remained at the base and read. That left three of us to "paint the town red"as the phrase went in those days. Neither of us had the paint nor the brush to do this. We were a humble group of warriors that hit town.

Female companionship was a good antidote for all our stresses and worries. We were quite shy and unaggressive and ended most evenings getting mellow on spirits finagled from a taxi driver or a hotel bellhop. The bombardier would sing lonely songs and I would try to help.

He talked about his girl at home and I did the same. At all

times, our waist gunner from Brooklyn lingered in the background looking after us. He was from a big city and wise in its ways. I was from the "sticks." The bomb aimer, though from a large city, spent most of his younger days playing music. We loved that fellow. Sometime, while working together, we unintentionally provoked him. He always had the same retort, "To hell witch youse." After distilling the numerous discussions between us, the bombardier and I concluded that in our lives we hadn't accomplished very much.

Came January 2, 1943, apparently the generals at last had come up with something. What it was we could not ever know. Our job was to "go and not ask why" as a famous poet put it.

No more were we to fly training planes. There was a brand new B24 in Pueblo, Colorado, waiting for us. We had to go there and fly it back. It would be ours for the duration. A plane of our own sounded great and was somewhat of a morale booster. What we were to do with it didn't tickle our minds for a while. Orders were to proceed at once.

It was a cold January 3 when we arrived at Operations. The airport was covered in fog mixed with freezing drizzle. The pilot questioned Operations about us being cleared to take off in these conditions. He was assured that if we quickly climbed to 8,000 feet, it would be clear flying all the way to Pueblo. Conditions there were much better for landing.

Eleven men would make the flight. We gained an extra pilot who would fly this plane along with our copilot. Our pilot would ride.

Our plane was within walking distance. We found it to be a very old machine. Probably, one of the first B24s manufactured. Its paint had chipped and peeled in many places. Its appearance indicated that it had flown many hours.

For a minute, our pilot and I stopped and gazed at the leading edge of the wing. Then he said, "Hmmm, no de-icers!"

I had an urge to say, "Let's not go up," but remained still. The pilot and I looked at each other, shook our heads, shrugged our shoulders, and crawled in. We had been cleared to go. So, ours was to go.

The pilot and copilot always had their parachutes installed in the cockpit seats while the remainder of the crew checked out theirs and carried them aboard. The parachutes were of two types, the chest type and the seat type. On this flight we were all issued the chest type.

So routine had flying become that numerous careless habits had slowly crept into our operational procedures. One such bad habit was throwing our chutes in through the waist gunner's window and going on about our business. There was little room for them where we worked, and they were often in the way.

I developed this habit after about a month-and-a-half of flying. In case of need, we thought we could all rush back and put them on. The fact that our bulky dress would snag on all manner of protuberances did little to itch our thoughts. Thus, we flew our tours. On this day I said to myself, almost aloud, "Dammit, I'm going to have my chute with me this time." I did not feel any special danger or fear. Many little things like no de-icers, the appearance of the plane, and the gloomy day probably added up to the caution. Anyway, I slammed my chute onto the navigation table. I was perturbed about the space it took.

I took out the charts and log, and prepared for takeoff. I logged the routine navigation tidbits, checked instruments, and wrote on a slip of paper the course to hand the pilot after we were airborne.

This time my position was in the nose compartment with the bombardier. Sometimes, we called this space the greenhouse, for it looked like one. In it was the bombsight and three of what I thought were the most useless, space robbing guns in the Army. Though they fired beautifully, one couldn't hit anything with them. At least, none of us could and we practiced a lot on easy straight-flying targets. They were situated wrong.

Takeoff was routine, though the conditions were somewhat harsh. The end of the runway was barely visible through the drizzle and light fog. We made one circle around the field using it as a point of departure and set course for Pueblo. I settled down to normal procedures that involved logging time, course, temperature, altitude, etc. The bombardier sat down and relaxed, no bombs.

Thoughts began to crowd into the cranium about the new aircraft that we would have and how soon we would soon be doing the modern version of the "charge of the Light Brigade." It matters not how modern warfare becomes, all men die the same way. The heart is caused to stop beating in hundreds of ways with the bullet that is no less painful than the arrow.

As usual, I monitored the navigation instruments for the course, the airspeed, and the time. Soon the time of arrival would be computed. This was important for we had to know when to start looking for our destination. The conditions outside were very soupy. It reminded me of flying through mashed potatoes.

Ice was forming on the nose and the temperature was dropping. My eye fastened on the altimeter. It read 5,000 feet and we'd been in the air for over ten minutes. Three thousand more feet and we should be flying in the clear. I thought we are not climbing fast enough. Should I tell the pilot to hurry it up? No, I decided. There was a man at the wheel who knew what he was doing. I became interested in the ice formations on the prop hubs. They were unusual in shape with a lump at the exact center and projections spinning out. Over the interphone I heard the pilot's voice speaking to someone, "Is this all we can get out of this thing?"

Then, someone from the rear said, "By gully, there is ice building up on the tail." More comments about ice on the tail followed. Some were calm and some a little concerned. "It's okay, we'll soon climb out of this into the clear. About a thousand more feet," came the pilot's voice.

I began to study the ice on the leading edge of the wing. It was getting heavier and heavier with spikes forming perpendicular to the plane of the wing. A big shudder developed over the whole airplane. It kept increasing and the boys in the rear began to jam the interphone inquiring about what was happening. The pilot's voice, "All right you guys, relax."

The shuddering increased, and we broke through the under cast into a beautiful clear sky, cold and blue above and brilliant rolling clouds below. The sun had a brilliant orange cast and was dead ahead. Instead of climbing higher, we skimmed along the surface of the clouds and sometimes through some that projected higher. The shuddering continued and anyone with dentures probably lost them.

The pilot tried to say something and someone in the rear yelled. All the pilot could say was, "Dammit."

The plane now plowed into the under cast. It did not emerge again. I had a hard time staying in my seat. The pencils, dividers, and loose navigation instruments slid off the table. I clamped my eyes on the altimeter and air speed indicator. Our speed was increasing while the altitude was decreasing at an alarming rate. "Ye gods," I said to myself, "these things could only indicate that we are flying straight down."

Without thinking, I clamped on my parachute. How mechanical this action was. In a second, the pilot rang the emergency bell that meant put on chutes and stand by. No jumping was to be done until he gave the abandon ship signal.

A great sensation of pressure surged through my brain, backbone, and heels. "He should be ringing abandon ship right now," I thought, and felt doomed. This happened to many others, so why not us? God does not grant privileges, he treats every one the same. I prepared to wait to see what dying was like.

Some strange force seized my body. I looked at the altimeter which was unwinding wildly. Some force propelled me toward the nose wheel door and the two red emergency handles. I yanked with all my strength. The doors flew open. I waited a second for a signal. None came.

A thought flew through my being, "You can't go now. You haven't accomplished anything." Then came a spilt second of confusion while the mysterious force gave me a boot out the door.

In the next instant, I noted that the big plane was spinning and whipping. This caused me to slip along the ship between the prop and the fuselage.

I pulled on the chute ring and it came out with a short length of cable. A malfunction! I felt doomed. I threw the ring violently away and looked up to a most beautiful sight. A gleaming white chute was opening up and blooming overhead. It had opened somewhere a little below the overcast.

A quick look away, I saw the B24 heading downward at a steep angle. It hit and exploded in flames, splashing gasoline over acres.

In two more seconds, I was zooming through a tall tree and hit the ground with a wham and a painful stab in one knee. A rabbit scurried away from under me. The branches of the tree pulled me off the ground about four feet and there I hung.

I looked at the plane's huge fireball as it rose into the overcast and disappeared about 500 feet up. A horrifying thought hit like a sledgehammer. There were eleven men in that fire. An impulse swept through my body to rush into the flames and pull them out. Then, came a paralysis producing realization that they were dead. I hung for some time with the heat from the fire hot on my face.

Upon later reflection, I estimated that the entire episode from the top of the overcast to the ground took no more that fifteen seconds.

In time the paralysis left, and I was cooling off. I freed myself from the chute and looked over to the fire and said, "To hell with flying. From the infantry I came and to infantry back I go. To hell with the commission."

With a painful leg, I limped to the plane. By that time, several dozen farm people had arrived and were throwing snow on burning bodies trying to put out the flames.

I stood and watched, numb. What was I to do? I knew I must go to the nearest phone and call. There were farmhouses in the distance. The farm people surrounded me and looked on with great sympathy. They were shocked and didn't know what to say.

Shortly, police from White City, Kansas, arrived and asked what needed to be done. All I could think of was the military way in disasters—post guards at the scene and call the commanding officer. The farmers were very helpful in every way. They called headquarters and arranged for my transportation back to the base.

Before I had left the scene, the sheriff arrived and told me that there was a big piece of something that looked like it might be from an airplane about a mile and a half down the road. He asked if I would go and identify it. Sure enough, it was a whole tail section of a B24, both rudders and the tail. The violent vibrations caused by ice resulted in the tail being ripped off. This probably occurred 6,000 feet above ground, and in 15 seconds or less we were down. The pilot, not knowing this, probably thought he could control the plane. The confusion on the interphones might have added a few seconds delay to important actions. The soup we were flying in did not help the pilot to ascertain our flying altitude. These conditions and the very short time available to make decisions added up to this disaster.

The police found a minister who drove 100 miles to Topeka to get me "home." I was gently and quietly examined, x-rayed, and placed in a hospital room. This was about four o'clock in the morning.

When alone at last, I pulled one hand from under the covers. For a while I gazed at it with a numb sensation. Here was a hand, warm and soft with feeling and circulation in it and able to move. How close it had come to being just the opposite jarred my whole being. Then, a good feeling slowly seeped through my body because I had survived.

Suddenly, there exploded a realization that my buddies were not so fortunate. I should have stuck with them to the end. Ashamed, I put the hand back under the covers. I was an unreliable member of this crew. How would I have performed in combat? Nothing was clear. The good feeling of survival scrambled with the feelings of a deserter who failed when his friends needed him most. I was one hell of a poor soldier. Surviving was worthless. Somewhere in this confused, inner combat, I plunged into slumber.

The Army medics were wonderful and seemed to know and understand my every problem. Here I developed a feeling about how valuable the country and the Army considers individuals and expends great efforts to rehabilitate those who are hurt. Complexities of why the nation drafts people and puts them into hazardous situations were too great to solve at this time. The dominant thought was to do the job as quickly as possible so we could go home.

I was left alone for a week in a Topeka Army hospital with every need met. Word came that another B24 crew was lost in an accident with no survivors. With time available, it was possible to wrestle with a number of thoughts and problems. The second B24 disaster sent a jarring fear of flying into my system. At that moment, I felt unable to go into the air again. I would disqualify myself come what may.

I asked, "Why did I get into the Air Corps at all?" I reflected on how in the infantry regiment, I studied flying service recruiting posters in the office and library. Enticing posters, they featured a goggled, handsome, steely-eyed defender standing in front of a large, four-blade propellered airplane, staring up at some distant object in the wild blue yonder. In the far background, several aircraft were zooming out of the clouds ready to challenge come what may. All this depicted fame, adventure, glory, heroism, great fun, and satisfaction. All this you could get if only you became a pilot. Just pass some tests and the rest would be as in the poster.

This enticing poster came out in November and December of 1941. I had about three months of Army service to go. Like most of the troops, I was counting days. The excitement promised in the posters received my scant attention. I vowed to serve my time in the infantry and get out.

One of my great disappointments in the service was that I was not assigned to an artillery unit. In college, one of the fascinating topics in higher mathematics was the study of projectile trajectories in resisting medias. I mastered this topic well. The word conveyed in all recruitment literature was that the Army would place you in units that your skills and qualifications dictated. Though my qualifications were duly noted in the records, they were by and large ignored. Hopes to work in an artillery unit went splat. Instead, I found myself digging foxholes in the infantry.

This I didn't mind for it was to be only one year and out. I was at a point where days to go were small numbers. Then, one Sunday evening on returning to the base from downtown, we heard loud speakers all over Camp Livingston blasting that Pearl Harbor had been attacked. Plans to go home after one year went up like a punctured balloon.

Next day, I dashed to the sergeant's tent to inquire about chances to transfer to the air corps. A number of us furnished him with literature indicating that anyone feeling qualified must be allowed to take tests, and if passed, must be allowed to transfer. He answered, "With this I cannot stop you from transferring out."

Thus, a few others and I became "Flying Cadets" as it was then called. I now had an opportunity to fly, be adventurous, be brave, be heroic, zoom to meet the thunder, be free. "To go down in flames," as the song went, met scant or no attention. Such is the rashness and the piss and vinegar of youth.

We gathered, thousands of us young ones, the flower of American youth, in a personnel pool in Colorado and waited. Almost to the last man, we were determined to be pilots. Only to pilots would all the adventurous goodies accrue. It was never so stated, but that is the way we felt after the conversations were distilled. The Air Corps was expanding rapidly and needed all kinds of flyers. Daily, we watched the bulletin boards where our pilot, navigator, or bombardier assignments were posted.

Pilot assignees went off satisfied, but for the other categories, well, "Orders is orders" was the common attitude, and we took it. I was to be a navigator, so be it. A feeling of determination surged in all my blood vessels.

Upon graduation, I would be a second lieutenant, something beyond my wildest aspirations when my military service began. When drafted, I knew next to zero about the armed services other then they had officers and peons and fought battles. I also knew that peons saluted officers, but how an officer differed from a peon I knew not.

I soon learned that not saluting an officer meant disciplinary action and all manner of bad things. The first day I put on my uniform I saluted a soldier who had one stripe on his sleeve. He looked different, I thought, so he must be an officer. Thus, began my military career. It was accompanied by all manner of jars and harsh episodes, all of which instilled a type of attitude where one, who is a private, does not ask questions or think, but does as told.

An incident on a street at Camp Livingston lingers in my

mind. A slip of paper was blowing across the sidewalk. I was tying my shoe when a corporal came by and saw the paper crossing in front of him. "Pick up this paper," roared the corporal. "In a second, as soon as I finishing tying my shoe," I answered. Then came the corporal storming, "Soldier, when I say do, you do and do right now. Get it? Right now! I'm putting you on report." I received extra K.P. and guard duty on the company street.

I was out of this now. I knew something of the Army and was on my way to a commission and what formerly seemed an unknown and forbidden world that it kept hidden. Navigation school lasted nine months and was no pushover for me. I felt like the second largest fish in the pond. If I didn't keep moving, I'd become some kind of casualty.

I was among a host of bright fellows from sophisticated backgrounds, little of which I could match. What I lacked in acuity I had to make up in determination and extra effort. Extra effort had always been my rescuing attribute. Something my father relied on to obtain what he had. He was a slow man with a great capacity to work long hours without relaxing to earn what others received quickly. My college years were also marked by the same problems that father had to face but on a different level.

In our training as navigators, great stress was given to "precision navigation." The system was derived, I believe, from sea navigation where speeds were 20 knots and crudely adapted to air navigation where speeds were 200 knots. A precise "fix" had to be obtained working in a cold, drafty, vibrating, pitching, dark, 200 mph aircraft. It had to be done in three minutes after consulting large, number tables and using a liberal amount of pencil work. Chances for error were rampant. When a frightened man did this in combat conditions, the results were often less than satisfactory. Thus, there were stories such as a bomber running out of fuel deep in an African desert when flying to a port on the Mediterranean coast, or a fleet of bombers missing the central Pacific fortress of Truk by a hundred miles. Yet, with this system we went to war and won.

Came October 2, 1942, and graduation from navigation school and a commission to second lieutenant. For me, it was a quantum jump both as a soldier and a man.

With a new uniform, I looked in the mirror and reflected. To mind came stories that dad would tell. At age 19, he fled Lithuania to escape the dreaded Russian Army. Lithuanians were then a subservient people and subject to Russian universal military service. Sons of peasants had no hope of ever aspiring to any rank above that of a private. Even sons of Russian peasants had only a slightly better chance to advance through the ranks. Sons of people of means had very little difficulty being promoted regardless of merit.

Here was I, a son of a peasant, with a commission. Impossible? This was another item that endeared me to this country, even though I had done my share of bitching over the wrongs I thought it had done to me.

We found ourselves in a giant pool of pilots, navigators, and bombardiers watching the boards for our names and assignments. Since the Air Corps was expanding explosively, we had a choice of aircraft we wanted to fly. From a choice of light bombers, medium bombers, heavy bombers, troop carriers, cargo carriers, and ferry command I chose heavy bombers. What could be more secure than flying in a "Flying Fortress?" I had heard very little about the B24 "Liberator."

In a few days, assignments came, and mine was to report to Tucson, Arizona, and the B24 Liberator heavy bomber unit. Again, it was not exactly the Flying Fortress that I had expected, but "orders is orders." I made an agreement with myself to be a good B24 navigator.

Days passed at the Topeka Army Hospital. Not being bothered by anybody nor pressured in any way, I began to calm myself into cooler thinking. I began to rethink about the fear of flying and what it was that I was afraid of. I thought that it was a fear of being killed. Well that's nothing unique. Whether flying or walking, everybody is afraid of being killed. Many of my best buddies had already died. What was the difference whether I walked or flew?

I began to be ashamed of ever harboring the thought of running after all my training. Besides, this was wartime. Also, as the result of receiving a commission and receiving good treatment at the hospital, some patriotic blood began to flow in my veins and arteries. Now, I felt that I owed something to the fine fellows who had died. Thus, I made a decision to go to the office and declare that I was ready for an assignment to another crew and to carry on from where I had left off. Otherwise, some other guy would have to make up for where I had failed. So far in life I hadn't accomplished anything, and this was a chance to begin. This was about the sixth day after the accident.

The flight surgeon and some kind of a psychologist examined me and asked all kinds of questions. Then they looked at each other. After a short pause and a mini-nod one of them said, "You will be cleared for flying in about three or four days. You are fine except that your knee needs more time to mend. After that, take it easy for about two weeks and you'll be good as new."

This was good news, but I felt a tinge of apprehension about flying again and eventually facing the dark gaping chasm of the uncertain and the unknown. Again, I went and stood before a mirror and reflected over the past and future. I thought about the plane crash I had survived. I remembered the disturbing thought I had as I was pushed through the escape door. "I haven't accomplished anything yet."

*Parachute of my first jump near White City, Kansas, January 5, 1943. The second chute was lost in the South Pacific, October 25, 1943.*

# Chapter 2

The isolated life I led from age three through high school, coupled with farming land that did not produce precluded me from living in the mainstream of the day. In any gathering of young people, whether in school or social affairs, the kids seemed to have done more, seen more, had more to laugh about, ate better, dressed better, and knew more than me. I didn't fare any better during the Depression. My folks didn't know how to seek relief from welfare agencies. The kids who enjoyed the benefits of welfare wore better clothes, carried better dinner pails, and ate goodies that I drooled over.

I started elementary school not knowing how to speak a word of English. The poor teacher did not quite know how to cope with my problem, but she managed to teach me "to barely speak English" at the end of the first year as she recorded in her reports. So during the first three years, until I was able to speak as well as the rest, I needed to overcome laughter from peers when I talked or read. As I got older and into high school, I discovered I was shy, reticent, and holding back.

Upon graduation from high school as class salutatorian, the superintendent summoned me to his office to talk about my future plans and aspirations. I said that I was uncertain, and had no plans other than going back to the farm with Mom and Dad. They were not doing so well.

The superintendent with eyes doubling in size stood up and said, "To heck you are! You are not going to the farm. Your folks will do all right because you will help them in a better way. You are going to college and that's that!"

I just said, "I am?"

He replied, "Yes. What college would you like to go to?"

I wiggled in my chair for some time until I remembered the college the superintendent himself went to and said, "Maybe I can go to Kalamazoo."

"Good," he said. "I know the dean and the registrar. I'll arrange everything. You get some money together. Do you have any idea where you might get a job?" Again, I wiggled in a sweaty chair and thought. "I can ask one of Dad's friends who works on the car ferries out of Ludington," I said.

"When do you plan to ask?" he asked.

"Maybe I will go to see him next week," I said.

"Hell you are!" he said. "You'll call him now. Here's the telephone. Call!"

I was shocked at such talk coming from the superintendent. I hunted for the number and called. The wife answered and said that her husband had mentioned a vacancy on a ship and would ask him about it that night.

My life assumed a strange and a totally unexpected direction. Two days after high school graduation I left for the steamboats, leaving poor Mom and Dad standing side by side with sad looks on their faces, within an inch of tears.

I fought tears myself thinking of the dashed plans Dad had made for the summer. We would have worked the stingy, stubborn, sandy land whose yield became more meager each passing year. As the yield diminished, Dad increased his effort to squeeze more from it. The farm was large, but the soil was sub marginal. But with my extra hands, more ground was to have been worked. Dad would not give in and Ma would push him.

They saw me through four years of college, selling a cow, and trapping extra muskrat and mink when tuition came due.

Mom and Dad had each spent three winters in school and

were able to read and write enough to get along. Russians discouraged Lithuanians from going to school so what education they had was acquired secretly.

At the end of my fourth year in college I received my draft number. Again, life took another direction.

★★★

The fact that I was now an officer gave me a mild jolt. A short nine months ago I had jumped at the bark of a corporal, and developed ways to survive in that world. Now my role had been completely reversed, and I could make the corporal jump. I must now learn to survive in a different world. I must shed my retiring, shy, and unassuming manner if I was to assuage the impulse that drove me out of the craft because, "I hadn't accomplished anything yet." It seemed that God figured that since "you haven't come across yet, I'll give you another chance."

I dated very few girls. In high school, I dated for the junior and senior proms. At college, I went to the dances when not working and dated for junior and senior proms. I had good times at these parties and enjoyed female companionship. But to "go steady" as was vogue, I did not do. I lacked that aggressiveness or forwardness. I missed the female companionship during weekends off base. This was something that would have afforded a more pleasant side of life in contrast to the study of bomb dropping.

At home there was a girl whom I had been fond of since childhood and thought about a great deal. Often I had looked for her at local dances and danced with her when I could. Once I drove to her home to take her out. Her mother said, "No!" I was determined to go back again, but the Army called me first.

She was much in my mind during the early military months, and I yearned to have her picture on my stand. I hesitated to ask for one fearing she'd say no. Now, however, with a resolve to change I said to myself, "Nuts with this attitude."

I sat down and wrote her a cautious letter. A friendly and proper response came. As time went on the feelings between us warmed, then flowered into something really uplifting.

Life took on a new complexion and looking forward to her letters became one of my fondest pleasures in these serious times. Before long, I received a large colored picture that sat prominently on my desk. The war was not so dark now. I had someone to visit with after duty. The war went on.

Just before discharge from the hospital and restoration of normal walk, I began receiving mail from families, friends, relatives, and sweethearts of the men who were lost in the crash. I was not prepared for this. These men were not just simply men alone, but also part of the parents and all manner of loved ones and friends. Each of these men had many who cared for them and were enduring a pain at their loss. Much more was lost than a man and his life. Between the lines, each letter begged some assurance that what had happened really hadn't happened and that it had been a mistake.

All begged for some bit of information about the last moments. What was said, how one looked, what one did, and the like. Above all, they wanted to hear that this must not have happened.

I was faced with a task of lifting as much grief as possible from folks in supreme sorrow. I wrote all day with hope that I was really "accomplishing something."

The mother of the pilot continued correspondence over years maintaining that I was now her son and that I would fill in her life all that her son would have had he lived. I had never had a humbler feeling. I promised to do all that I could.

I was given a seven-day sick leave upon discharge from Topeka Army Hospital. On the way home I stopped at the home, of the bombardier's parents. I do not know if I did the proper thing, for it seemed that upon seeing me their grief and tears started all over again. The wound was opened again. They showed me his grave that was just across the street and in plain sight from the living room window.

His mother said, "See, he will always be with us now. They'll never take him from us again." Then she burst into tears. I stood helpless.

At home Mom and Dad did not know how to react to me, knowing what had happened. Dad was silent for a long time, and finally asked if this war was necessary. Mom hugged me for a long time. Later, we chatted for hours.

After sick leave, I flew by commercial plane to Tucson Army Air Base to start over. Men who were to make up the crew were already there, and I was the last to arrive.

The aircraft commander was a swarthy bloke with a confident manner. He assembled us as soon as we all arrived, and had us introduce ourselves and give our background. We seemed to like each other right away.

Because I had survived a plane crash, this training took on a grimmer aspect. I looked at our crewmembers, all young and vigorous and some just out of high school. They were not just isolated individuals, but men with all manner of connections with friends, parents, and sweethearts at home. A disaster with any one meant a disaster with many. As training accelerated, bonds of kinship developed and grew stronger. We were becoming a unit, some kind of a "fightin' machine" which these times needed.

The bombardier and I turned out to be very similar fellows; similar in temperament, demeanor, tastes, and attitudes. The pilot was way ahead of us in aggressiveness and oral suavity. He had a great advantage over us with the ladies. The copilot was somewhere behind him, but ahead of the bomb man and I.

Life was not all studying war. Weekends were usually free and sometimes there was a pause during the week. Sometimes we even ran short of fuel and paused.

During each hiatus, the bombardier and I trundled toward the bright lights of Tucson with the object of diluting our woes with wine, ladies, and music. Neither of us liked alcohol, but nevertheless partaking of it seemed like an appropriate thing to do. So we took a shot or so, but only to a point where a feeling of wisdom and boldness began to stir in our veins. These were emergency times we rationalized.

One particular evening the bombardier and I went to a nightclub in town for rehabilitation and solace. After the usual preliminary ritual of building up wisdom and confidence, we were ready for a real jolly time. There played an unusual little band pumping out such tunes as "The Hutsut Song," "Three Little Fishes," "A Tisket a Tasket," "Mares Eat Oats and Does Eat Oats," and "Yellow Rose of Texas," all of which made youth surge in our veins.

We both danced more than ever before and even enticed a lady away from our pilot. But alas, the eleventh hour came and all GI's had to be off the streets and on base. The bombardier had left a half hour earlier. The young lady and I were alone, except for numerous civilians.

The last bus had left. There was no transportation to the base. Not being on base on time meant a 1943 military version of turning into a pumpkin. I explained the dilemma to the young lady who immediately said, "Take me home and you may use my auto."

From then it was a rush to beat the eleventh hour. Tucson was a sizable city and she guided me to her home by directions, turn here, turn there, turn this way or that way until she said, "Here it is." After a hurried, standard ceremony of seeing her to the door, I sped to the base and arrived just in time.

It wasn't until the next morning that questions boomed in my mind. What was the girl's name? Where did she live? What was her address? How would I return the car? Neither of us had given the other our name.

Another panicking thought—What if she, out of fright, reported that some GI officer had stolen her car? I could not return it at once, for I knew not where to, and there was a full day of Uncle Sam's obligation to fulfill first.

The day passed routinely. Every minute I hoped that no night flying would be scheduled. Fortunately none was.

I smoked back to the nightclub as early as possible. There stood the young lady who looked as though she'd worried for 24 hours. She spilled out the whole story of her woe and how she had to keep the truth from her dad who had queried about the car's whereabouts. Only by her quick wit was she able to calm her father. We both relaxed and introduced ourselves.

Then she said, "Let's not go to the night club. Let's go to my home and spend the evening with my folks." Very quickly I said, "Yes."

She introduced me to her parents who were very friendly. Then she said, "My Dad is a sheriff in this town." I hid my tremendous astonishment but should have guessed from the accouterments and memorabilia about the house.

Later the sheriff asked, "Do you like tequila?"

I said, "I never tasted it."

Then he said, "Let me give you some. I have the best." We took a shot. Then more. And still more. The taste was not much to my liking. He was a very nice man, and he had a very nice daughter. That compensated for the dubious taste.

Mother came in with some strange new goodies. Thus we spent the evening, talking war and drinking. The tequila was very effective.

Suddenly, Dad and Mom left saying, "You two can visit now. We'll retire." The eleventh hour came too soon and with it the fearful specter of the military version of the big pumpkin.

This second time through the first phase in B24 training seemed to go much faster than the first. Thirty days and it was over. Our pilot did unusually well, learning quickly. We became very confident that with him our chances for survival were very good.

For second phase work, we airlifted to Alamogordo, New Mexico, where the bombardier was to learn his trade in this particular aircraft. After two weeks, we were ordered out of Alamogordo and into Biggs Field, El Paso, Texas.

There was more to do for crews during this phase than the previous time through. We spent longer hours at work. When not flying, officers fine-tuned their skills in simulators, such as link trainers, navitrainers and bomb simulators. The gunners sharpened their eyes on numerous ground-mounted gun turrets. The pressure was on.

One day another disaster visited our unit. We lost a bomber and crew. From evidence gathered, it was concluded that the crew accidentally flew into a huge vertical, turbulent, cumulus cloud. Because of violent currents within the cloud, the airplane broke up. It fell from the bottom of the cloud and scattered over a wide area of the white sands of Alamogordo. One of the bodies recovered was a Michigan boy. Since I was from that state I was asked to escort the body home and represent the Air Corps.

It was almost a three-day trip by slow train to Detroit. I was not very well briefed on the particulars of either the accident or how to handle people in extreme grief.

The relatives begged for answers on how their much-loved boy was killed and why this was allowed to happen. To these questions I could give only vague answers. The people responded with anger as though I had sent the crew up into the weather in a faulty plane.

I spent a miserable day not being of much help. However, I seemed to calm their frustrations somewhat by assuring them that the Air Corps was very safety conscious and did not carelessly send up crews in defective airplanes. This was an unforeseen accident, like those with automobiles or machinery.

The parents of the boy were, like myself, Lithuanians. They were in their early 70s and had this son, who was now 20, late in life. He was their only child. The father resembled my own Dad. He showed evidence of a youth full of hardships and had the bowed shoulders and massive hands indicative of heavy labor. I learned that most of his life in America had been spent digging coal.

The mother matched her husband. All about her indicated the struggle to make a little go a long way. Late in life they had moved from the coal country to Detroit, bought a decent house, and began to accumulate some of the nicer things — all of which they planned to "leave to our son so he can have it better."

During the whole time, the father sat motionless in his chair, his head bowed, staring at the floor. He moved when someone took him by the hand and led him around. The mother clawed at the sealed casket crying, "I want to see him once again, I want to see him."

The relatives calmed her with difficulty and held her. I stood tearfully by, angry that I couldn't do anything.

The slow train ride back to El Paso gave me time to think. The scene I had observed was being repeated nine times throughout the country and this was only an "at home" accident. We had not yet been in heavy air fighting. The thousands of crews we were now training would shortly collide with an opposing counterpart who were now preparing as we were.

I reviewed the experience I had just had in Detroit. Would I cause my own parents to go through an episode like it? I must not. Good Fortune had eluded them at almost every turn in their lives. Any more would be unfair.

Dad came to this country in 1907 in a move to escape service in the Russian Army. Most of his countrymen gravitated to the Pennsylvania coalmines because that's where the jobs were and labor was all they had to offer. Dad found work in the flourmills in Niagara Falls at 10 cents per hour, 10 hours a day. He felt himself to be most fortunate because in Lithuania a young man was lucky to find work with a land baron at $15 per year. Here he would be earning that much in 15 days and in fewer hours. In the old country, starting hour was sunup, and quitting time was sundown. For women, sundown did not mean that the day's work was over, for spinning wool and linen then began.

Mother was happy when she obtained a job making spoons in a silverware factory for 10 hours a day at 10 cents per hour.

After Mom and Dad married, they felt that at last they had a chance to prosper. Good fortune was shining upon them.

In time, wages were raised to 15 cents per hour, which added to their happiness and satisfaction. Still, Dad was a man who grew up working the soil and to the soil he longed to go. Finally, an ad in a Lithuanian newspaper caught his eye about a land deal he couldn't resist. In Mason County, Michigan, were 480 acres of land within reach of his budget. The real estate agent was Lithuanian and the area was heavily inhabited with his countrymen. He couldn't go wrong.

The agent helped with train fare to examine the land. It was virgin land, not cleared of stumps from recently cut over forest. There was a house and barn on it, and a large lake. The soil looked light and sandy. To a trained farmer's eye it betrayed a short productive life. To Dad it mattered not for there was a lot of it. In the country of his youth, big families subsisted on small plots and farmed every square inch of it. Here he would work vast areas. He bought the farm with the help of the agent and the bank.

The virgin land was productive. Dad was overjoyed and visualized a bright future. The stumps proved to be an annoying nuisance that he had to eliminate. He began a program of stump pulling, which by the end of 10 years produced 40 acres of cleared land. When we were not planting or harvesting, we were stump pulling.

There were other Lithuanian farmers in the area with whom we associated and made music together. Some were in the same predicament as we, but most were on good land already cleared. When their children took a respite or went fishing we were pulling stumps. As time went on and more stumpy land was cleared, the ground already cleared became less productive. To Dad, this meant that more land had to be cleared. So with increased determination, we pulled more stumps.

I had to keep up with him and marveled at his persistence and endurance. He never worked fast, but he moved long. He would say, "Work slow and you will work a long time." I developed a feeling that this was a proper way of life, and that anyone who did less was in the wrong. If a task took a long time, then take a long time.

Mother did not reconcile herself to Dad's slow gait, but could do little to speed him up. However, she was a good supplement to Dad. She was quick and efficient, and took charge of all manner of miscellaneous tasks. Ducks, geese, chickens, sheep, turkeys, and such were her areas of responsibility. She sheared sheep, spun wool, and knitted sweaters for all of us.

Half way through the stump era, my first sister was born. Seven years later my second sister was born. By now, Dad's tenaciousness began to wane. He gave up trying to eke less and less from more and more. He sold the place for whatever it could bring and bought 120 acres of much better land. He began to prosper moderately,

After some reflection on his new situation, he finally said to me, "Ne bouk tokis razumnas kaip muzikas po laiki." This may be roughly translated as, "Don't be too soon old and too late smart."

He was even stashing away extra money and often refraining from things he needed. When I asked why he was sacrificing thus he replied, "It will not go for naught. You kids will enjoy it." He loved his kids. Mother, too, worked as hard for her kids.

In time, I reached college age and left the farm. Before I could return, the war had broken out and I was drafted.

★★★

I reported back at Bliss Field to find an order to be part of a special crew and to report the next morning to the commander at Hamilton Field, California. The crew was to consist of pilot, copilot, two navigators, and five observers. It seemed strange—two navigators, but no bombardier! We speculated that it would be a long, clandestine journey somewhere to spy on something. We went in great haste.

At Hamilton Field, we wondered why four such crews would participate in the project. We learned that two bombers had gone down between Hawaii and San Francisco, and that the crews were on rafts sending periodic signals. We were to fly a thousand miles, find them, and drop survival equipment. This was to sustain them until surface help arrived.

Four B24 bombers were to cover a narrow, wedge-shaped sector and at the end of the thousand miles conduct a square search for about half-an-hour. The square search involved flying increasing concentric squares until a designated area was fully searched. Without rest, we were ordered to take off.

It was almost sunup. With great haste, the two navigators laid out a course, marked off 100-mile intervals, noted compass deviation at each interval, and times to correct it. We were ready.

We knew something of the pilot. He had a reputation of not trusting navigators because he had been lost by one. We hoped he wouldn't argue with us about directions. Both of us navigators checked on each other and agreed on the courses and corrections.

Flying in the United States there were radio aids to rescue pilots when navigators went awry. Over oceans as vast as the Pacific, radio aids were not adequate. This was our first flight over such a long over-water course, and we were apprehensive after departure. It would be 12 hours before we saw land again. If we made any serious mistakes, it would not be known until after 12 hours.

For six hours, we flew toward the assigned search area. The plane was on autopilot and the two of us navigators made course corrections and kept checking our position by sun measurements. The pilot kept asking if our calculations were correct.

In the search area, we flew the predetermined square pattern with nine pairs of highest acuity eyeballs scanning the waters.

The desire to find the lost ones was very strong. We discussed going over the area again, but the matter of fuel precluded the attempt.

In this area of the Pacific the earth's magnetic field caused the compass to vary 45 degrees from north. This had to be corrected. Time came to head for San Francisco, and the other navigator and I together computed a compass heading for our return. The compass reading we gave the pilot was something like 355 degrees after all corrections. Upon hearing this the pilot's mistrust boomed. "Jesus Christ, what are you trying to feed me. Don't you want to get back? I know that San Francisco is northeast and something like 45 degrees you should be giving us. Your course will take us to Alaska and we won't get there!"

I was now concerned and looked at my co-worker for assurance. He said, "This is it."

I called, "We haven't time to argue. Come down and we'll go over this together."

We both explained the problem after which he said, "All right. Remember, if you goof, it's your ass."

After 10 hours of flying, the crew in the rear began to get restless and worried. They'd seen nothing but water all day. "What's our time of arrival?" they asked.

"Two-and-a-half more hours," we'd reply.

"Are you sure?" they would ask.

"Yes," we would say.

"How do you figure it?" some one would comment. "You saw nothing but water all day. Come on now!"

We noted the pilot fiddling with the radio compass but nothing yet. Too far away. This sort of commentary went on until we sighted San Francisco and the radio compass pointed straight ahead. Someone in the top turret yelled, "Land ho!" and all interphones became silent. We navigators whose tensions had been building up sighed relief. It had been 13 hours of flight.

On landing, both pilots shook our hands and the observers made nice compliments. We turned in our logs and charts. After checking them over the commander said, "You guys didn't loaf up there, did you?" Upon our charts were plotted dozens of sun lines and sun fixes. We knew we were on course. In four days we flew three such flights, each between 14 and 15 hours long. When we returned to El Paso, we were exhausted.

In the midst of our training, our pilot became ill and was sent to Colorado for treatment. We were now a crew without a leader. His treatment would not be long we were told. The thought that we would resume as a crew upon his return made us happy.

In the meantime, we worked on our respective simulators. One evening while filling my supper plate, a courier rushed up to me and handed a large sealed envelope with "SECRET" stamped in red all over it. "Open at once," he said and left. In it was an order from some high headquarters signed by a general to proceed at once to San Francisco by quickest possible means, military or commercial. I was to report to the commander in order to participate in some project like AB2D. It stressed, "at once."

Our base commander knew about this and was already arranging a commercial carrier. I couldn't eat. "What in the world could this be," I wondered.

I began to visualize another one-way Dolittle type raid with B24s from Alaska or another distant point from Japan. We would carry one 500 pound-bomb and three bomb bay tanks of fuel that would give us a range of close to 3,000 miles. Otherwise, why would such an order be classified secret? There was tension, excitement, fear, and wonderment in my body.

So it was that for a second time in a week I was at San Francisco's Hamilton Army Air Base. I reported and braced for a shocking blow. It turned out the navigator of a crew that was about to take off across the Pacific had had a nervous breakdown and could no longer fly. During training his performance was such that the crew lost confidence in him and wanted someone else. The Army scrounged about and picked me.

The crew was already in the ready room of operations when I first met them. The first words of the pilot, after introduction, were, "Are we ever glad to see you." After introducing each member we sat down for a snack. Then I asked, "How come you are happy to have me on the crew when you don't know anything about me?"
The pilot said, "We were shown your work during the sea search you did last week. We liked it and asked for you."

Thus, I became an instant navigator of a new crew. Since I had flown all night to arrive there, I was allowed to rest after a briefing for the departure next morning. Since the rest of the day was free, we spent it becoming acquainted.

The pilot looked like the youngest man on the crew. He could have easily passed for a sophomore in high school and he did not own a razor. During summer he helped his father farm. He attended a college in Oregon where he had completed two years.

The copilot, after a few minutes, revealed a congenial nature. "He and I will stick together like a hip pocket to a pair of pants," I thought. The first thing one noticed was that he was short! In a conversation that developed he said, "I'm not certain you noticed my altitude. Let me give you the particulars. At the first physical for the Flying Cadet Corps I was rejected—too short! However, a sergeant took me aside and explained a series of stretching exercises whereby I could increase my height by the quarter-of-an-inch I was lacking. He told me to return in 30 days. I hung and stretched for hours for a month and then returned. They recognized me, looked at my previous exam records, and said I was okay. They accepted me without even measuring. I was PO'd." The country obtained another good pilot.

The bombardier was a thin-faced youngster with thick, short, dark hair and one cheek slightly puffed from years of chewing tobacco. An accent in his speech was such that from his first, "How are yah?" I gathered he was from the Deep South. He worked on the railroad about which he was always ready to discourse.

The flight engineer resembled a Lithuanian but was Polish. He seldom talked without laughing and often just laughed.

The radio operator was as sober and reticent as the engineer was jovial.

Probably the oldest member of the team was the ball turret gunner. He had pronounced creases from his Roman nose to around his mouth. In my opinion, his job was the most frightful, but he seemed quite pleased with it.

A jolly fellow a bit shorter than our copilot was the youth whose career was to man the nose turret. A story he would sometimes tell went something like this, "I got into a fight with some jerk once. He looked down at the top of my head. I looked straight ahead into his belly button. We growled back and forth until I got really mad. Then I hauled off and hit himright in the knee caps."

A round, dark haired, dark completed boy of Mexican origin was the tail turret operator.

For waist gunners we had two redheaded kids just out of high school. These were the guys I was to live with and go to war with.

Before retiring, I studied the course to Hawaii. I plotted it and marked off 100-mile intervals and indicated course corrections and time of arrival at each interval.

The flight would be 2,100 nautical miles and 13 hours of estimated flying time. "Wow," I thought.

While still in grade school, I read with excitement and thrill about Lindbergh's flight across the Atlantic, and later the opening of the trans-Pacific air service by "China Clipper" seaplanes. Having read about the feat by Columbus and the trials of the Mayflower, I viewed the crossing of oceans by airplanes as achievements of super brave supermen. Their miraculous machines of unimaginable speeds made crossings in hours that Columbus or Darwin did in months or even years.

Operating Dad's stump puller, I wondered how I happened to be so unfortunate as to never be able to accomplish big things like that. I thought I'd never be able to touch or even see people who were achievers like trans-Pacific fliers.

In Dad's and Mom's world, most people were born, lived out their lives and died without ever going more than five miles from their homes. So at the age of about 12, I gave in to dreaming about the big world with big men, doing big things somewhere far away, but never expecting to do more myself than till some sandy soil hoping for something to grow. Dreams were small and getting smaller. Now, fortune and misfortune were staring at me. Fortune, that I would be navigating across a big ocean. Misfortune, that I was headed toward war. "How come God created an opposite to every good thing that he created?" I asked myself." Will I always have to suffer a misfortune for every success?"

Just before sunrise in mid-May of 1943, our giant Liberator roared down the runway. It was loaded to capacity. Of the four bomb bays, two were loaded with 300-gallon fuel tanks. The remaining two were packed to the ceiling with mailbags. I looked at all that mail and thought about the GIs who were expecting it. "By golly, we better deliver," I thought to myself.

After we cleared the runway and gained a little altitude, the prison of Alcatraz loomed straight ahead. I immediately felt an urge for mischief. "Let's fly low and slow over it and see what happens," I called to the pilot with the understanding that flying over prisons was illegal.

"Let's, ha, ha, ha," said the pilot and we flew low and slow over Alcatraz. Nothing happened.

The Golden Gate Bridge was our point of departure. "Should we fly under it?" I asked the pilot.

"Very tempting if we longed to fight this war in a way other than how we are about to," said the pilot.

With this brief interlude of mischief over, I logged the departure time over the bridge and we headed across the Pacific to Hawaii. The sun, big and orange, lit up San Francisco. The eastern horizon was brilliant. The western horizon was still black with a dark haze over it. It felt like a bad omen. We were actually flying from the land of brightness and life toward darkness and gloom.

# Chapter 3

We settled on course. From here on there wasn't much to do except watch the compass and keep the altitude. The navigators position had been shifted from in front of to behind the pilot. This resulted in much less working space, but easier communication with the pilot.

I climbed into the upper gun turret. It was plexiglass which gave an excellent all-around view. I gazed back toward our departure. There was my country in the distance, rapidly receeding. Melancholy descended and enveloped my soul. Back there was my family, sweetheart, friends, and the sandy soil. Would I see them again?

I watched until land could be seen no more. Then I went back to the charts. I made measurements on the sun and plotted a few sun lines of position that gave a reasonable speed. From this I computed a preliminary time of arrival of 13 hours from departure.

From the relocated navigator's position, my view of the outside was limited to a foot square window to the left of the chart table and the astrodome through which sun and star observations were made. I looked at the engines and the spinning props and listened to the hum.

I began to feel strong warmth for the airplane. I thought, "This is the machine that will take us into harms way, endure wounds, and bring us safely back. This is our machine. We are a part of it and it is part of us. The airplane and the crew are one. It will bring us back over the Golden Gate Bridge and deposit us safely."

In six hours, we were again flying over the same area I covered a week earlier. Almost out of habit, I scanned the ocean in all directions. It is truly difficult to imagine how vast the Pacific is until one has to cross it.

After ten hours, the crew began to be interested in our progress and seemed anxious as to our position. Never before had they been so long without sight of land and wondered when we would arrive. Without benefit of charts, they did not have the true picture of our position. Soon the mountain on the main island of Hawaii began to show in the distance south of our course. The men cheered. During the 13th hour we landed at Hickam Field, Oahu.

Here, during the three weeks it took to modify our plane to meet new combat conditions, we isolated ourselves from the war and the world.

This was May of 1943, and it was the first chance I'd had to sit around and do nothing since February 1942. We visited our plane every day. The remainder of the day, we went swimming on Waikiki Beach. The beach was covered with GIs from every service.

I recalled a movie named "Waikiki Song." It featured numerous beauties in scant apparel doing romantic things and making music on the exciting Waikiki Beach. It had seemed like a place unreachable to any but people of great affluence. Now, here were sons of muzhiks, peons, peasants as well as the oppulent cluttering the beach. I experienced such fascination that, for a long time, I just stood and gazed.

In the evening, we were entertained by native dancing girls and endulged ourselves at big smorgasbords.

At the end of a week the bombardier remarked, "It soon ceases to be fun if all you can do is look but never touch." The copilot argued that beauty is beautiful all the time.

The pilot said, "Well, daylight is more pretty after a dark night." I couldn't make a connection in this situation. He then said, "If you worked in a coal mine all day you would see ten times more beauty in this than you do now." I didn't argue.

Our plane was pretty much dismantled and rebuilt. The greenhouse nose section was removed and a turret installed. A ball turret was installed in the belly replacing the one fired by periscope. In our training, radar was sometimes mentioned but our use of it seemed remote. Our airplane was to have radar installed. I was quite excited after hearing the magical things it could do.

In the third week the job was completed. We took classes in how to operate the new equipment, flew some orientation flights, and christened the plane "Big Moose." We all agreed on the name even though it had no connection to our lives.

A large head of a moose was painted on the side. We looked at it with pride. This was "our" airplane. Most crews named their planes after some lady like "Fanny Mae" and painted her scantly clothed. Some used their sweetheart's names or their mother's. We had Big Moose.

In the first week of June 1943, we received orders to depart for Canton Island about 1700 miles south and west of Hawaii. One crewman looked at the chart after I plotted the course and said, "Sir, are you sure that isn't a fly speck?" Indeed it was a small place. We arrived overhead in ten hours. It had a lot of sand and only one tree.

The following day we received orders to takeoff for the Fiji Islands about 1,100 miles west. There, we waited a week for orders.

The place was weighted down heavily with all types of GIs. Troops of other services contrasted sharply with flying units. Their camps were brightly lit with noisy, singing, yelling troops. Ours was dark and the troops sang no songs. We stayed in tents near our planes which looked like ominous giant monsters at night.

Finally, we were cleared for an 800-mile flight to New Caledonia where we waited for directions. There in the harbor was a fleet of warships, some showing battle scars. For the first time we began to show signs of excitement and anxiety.

Until this time, little was said about the war. If we thought about it, we did not discuss it, nor did any of us follow the press very closely. Within B24 range from New Caledonia was the big fight. We speculated as to where our base of operations would be.

One possibility was to proceed to Austraila and from there strike the Japs on New Guinea to the north. The other was to fly north to New Hebrides, then to newly secured Guadalcanal and raid westward.

During our stay in New Caledonia, we went to a town called Numea. It was a medium-sized town similar to ours in the 1890s. Unique however were women carrying parcels, large clay jars of liquids, and other heavy objects on their heads. They even carried heavy shopping baskets from town several miles to their homes in the countryside. "That's using their heads," said the copilot. The rest of us said, "Heh, heh, heh."

In late June orders arrived to fly 400 miles northward to New Hebrides. Upon briefing, we learned that we were to be early members of the newly formed 13th Air Force and that our unit would be the 372nd Squadron of 307th Bomb Group, Heavies. We would fly strike missions from Carney, a new air strip on Guadalcanal.

Before going there, a heavy schedule of formation flying would be completed. In mid-July, we made a 600-mile journey to Guadalcanal and established ourselves at a newly built facility for heavy bombers.

Headquarters, the operations building, and living quarters were long, camouflaged, round-roofed buildings set into the woods to hide them from aerial view.

Our hut held about 40 officer crew members. We slept on folding canvas cots covered with a blanket. There was no mattress. Everything we possessed was carried in one large bag and one military-type folding suitcase. We settled down to a new life, with deep meditation at the outset.

Next day, the commander conducted an all squadron briefing to familiarize us with the situation in our sphere of operations. According to reports, the Japs had lost Guadalcanal but were determined to recapture it. In preparation, they were reinforcing the islands to the west. Jap troops were being rushed to Bougainville, Vella Lavella, New Georgia, and Choiseul.

A landing strip was being built in great haste on New Georgia at a place called Munda. From there, about 150 miles from Guadalcanal, they would be able to raid U.S. facilities around the clock. Airfields on Bougainville were restocked with large numbers of new aircraft. It added up to a promise of a summer of fireworks.

Our function was to dissuade the Japs from prosecuting their design by conducting incursions over their facilities and depositing ordinance. We would not only defend Guadalcanal, but attack and occupy islands westward across the Solomons and beyond. This was the "big picture" in our corner of the world.

New crews were not suddenly plunged into combat operations. Members were parceled out, one to a bomber, to fly with veteran crews as observers to get a feel for what combat is like.

In the first week of August 1943, our crew made its first

combat raid. We were assigned to strike at Kahili Air Base on Bougainville, one of the more powerfully defended fields in the Solomons. I was the eleventh man on an experienced crew and was given the task of observing operations.

Strikes were timed to hit targets at any hour of the day. This one was timed so that the bombs were to be dropped at sunset. It usually took four hours to take off, assemble in squadrons and groups, pick up fighter escorts, fly to the target, and drop the bombs. To strike Buka Air Base at the far end of Bougainville took an hour longer.

Though it was a hot and steamy day, we were advised to take along winter flying clothing. Even in the tropics the temperature dropped rapidly with altitude. At 24,000 feet it was between 40 and 50 degrees below zero Fahrenheit. Even in the warmest wear the Air Corps could furnish, we shivered.

This flight consisted of three squadrons of about 9 to 12 planes each. To confuse the enemy as to where we would strike, the course consisted of several doglegs over the ocean; out of sight of any land where observers might be present and give a warning.

We approached Kahili from due north. In the distance and in the shadows of the setting sun, we spotted the white coral runway. In seconds, clouds of coral dust began to rise as Jap fighters scrambled.

Every muscle in my body became tight and tense. Deep in the recesses of the cranium lurked fear and an impulse to hide. Shivering from the cold ceased. Outer calm fought to hide inner turbulence.

With much deliberation, I forced myself to take note of what was happening to the altitude, speed, temperature, pilot's reactions, open bomb bays, bombs, hands of the top turret gunner, the navigator, the clock. This helped me to be calm.

The pilot began to grip the wheel with a force of a vise, while over the inner phones the gunners reported bogies to each other with altered voices.

Time to bombs away would be 10 to 15 minutes. I wanted to speed up the approach so we could get the hell out. Never had time seemed so slow. It had entered a conspiracy with the Japs to do us ill.

I recalled Einstein's comment about sitting on a hot stove for a minute that seemed like an hour. This thought was calming. To myself I said, "You are going to do this at least 25 times. Get used to it."

I went back to watching the drama when the top gunner fired a long burst. Spent shell casings cascaded all over the compartment and covered the navigator's table. I had my head in the astrodome scanning the sky.

Our plane was in the third element of three and on the right side. We were the leading squadron. Over the phone the bombardier said, "Bombardier to pilot, I.P. in about 15 seconds."

The pilot said, "Roger." I.P. meant initial point, a location on the ground over which the bombardier began the bomb run and flew the plane with the bomb sight.

Bomb runs generally lasted three to five minutes depending on altitude. They were the longest intervals of time in human experience. Tension coupled with a sense of no motion when flying at high altitudes tricks the time senses. Only by closely watching the clock could one stay tuned to reality.

The gunners began firing short bursts almost continuously.

From my position I could not see their targets. I wanted badly to see, so I planted myself between the pilots and had a pilot's view.

Black puffs began to pop all over. Suddenly, a huge white puff burst dead ahead with white streamers shooting downward. This was a surprise. I never heard of anything like that. Our formation flew under and beyond the phenomenon. The sight of the black puffs was horrifying.

After the initial point, the bomber must fly straight and level regardless of AA fire and fighters. This is truly a modern version of the "Charge of the Light Brigade."

Came the bombardier's voice, "Five seconds till." The pilot replied, "Roger." I positioned myself over the edge of the bomb bay and watched 20 hundred-pounders drop out at quarter second intervals.

I saw strings of bombs from other B24s accompanying our own. I felt exhilarated.

Then I had a sober thought. "These things will fall on people down there. I shouldn't be happy." Then came a jolt of reality. There on the ground sparked brilliant white flashes, seemed like hundreds of them, all around the runway and the jungle. Every flash meant a shell coming at us from underneath.

Through my mind flashed the most horrifying thought of all. Sitting on the edge of the bomb bay I visualized a shell coming through the underside of the plane, through my rectum and exploding. The event seemed so imminent that I jumped up violently nearly destroying the oxygen tube.

After a seemingly very long time, we were over the ocean again speeding toward lower altitude. The crescendo of firing increased while the gunners yelled to each other, "Get him Jack, Jesus Christ, Jack get him!" A hundred miles out at sea and at an altitude of 5,000 feet, the firing stopped and darkness enveloped.

The formation loosened up and finally scattered in the darkness. The crew began to communicate with their normal voices and I felt like a boiled noodle. I was cold but still sweated. The calmness and relaxation that settled over me was such that it was hard to suppress a yell. I knew what Churchill meant when he said, "There is nothing more gratifying than to be shot at and missed."

We felt that for the day our job was done. Time to go home and sit down for supper. We had been airborne for eight hours, most of it at high altitude on oxygen.

Before landing came a radio alarm, there were bogies accompanying us. We were told not to land but to circle Savo Island until all was clear. The bombers were low on fuel. As we formed a circular pattern over Savo, the bogies bombed a ship and straffed our landing strip. Others circled and waited for us to land.

Once again tension and a waiting game. Eventually, one of our bombers, low on fuel, had to land regardless of the Japs. Perhaps the Japs, too, were down on fuel. They made haphazzard passes over the plane, emptied their guns, and went home.

The first incoming bomber, however, was severely shot up by our own anti-aircraft gunners. Fortunately, no crew member was hit.

The rest of the squadrons were soon cleared to land. At final count one B24 did not return. It had disappeared into the darkness after its bomb drop.

After each raid, there was the standard, ritual debriefing conducted by the unit's intelligence officers. Experiences and observations of every crewman were noted and recorded. From this information, future action and tactics were developed.

After ten hours of non-stop action from wake-up to debriefing we ended mission number one for our crew. It was over. Every man was physically exhausted and emotionally drained.

We shuffled to the long, steamy, gloomy huts. A string of 15-watt bulbs fought with the darkness of our cave-like room. There was very little sound from the three dozen fatigued vocal cords.

After about half-an-hour of horizontal, our nerves thawed and one by one we slowly became vertical. We were hungry, and a hot meal was announced over the speakers.

The dining room soon became filled with closely packed bobbing heads. All was silent except for the clinking of silverware against the plates. This meal, as all meals in this corner of the world, consisted of canned and dehydrated food. All that could be dehydrated was. All that could be canned was. We learned to "love" powdered eggs, potatoes, milk, and vegetables. Meat, butter, bacon, beets, and such were canned. We ate these when there was no alternative.

Slowly voices began to pop up here and there. Before long, a crescendo of animated conversation flooded the room. It drowned out the earlier tapping of knives and forks. Men have the capacity to be happy over many things. This time they were happiest about being able to eat one more meal. There were ten men missing from the dining room this night.

We were quite well briefed about the situation in our immediate area. The Japs were stung about the loss of Guadalcanal, and began to reinforce the remainder of the Solomons with eventual plans to recapture Guadalcanal. They had an intense dislike and loathing for losing. Their armies never lost and never surrendered. It was simply not in their books. Any setbacks were only temporary. There was no such thing as a Japanese prisoner. Their soldiers either won or died.

Our objective was to see that they did lose, that their losses would be permanent, and that there would be many prisoners. We would hit them hard and often. For the first time, we had ample B24s, as well as B25s and numerous fighters.

The Army and Marines would also attack the Solomons at places called New Georgia, Munda, Vila, Kolombangara, Choiseul, and Bouganville. We would now begin to take and hold. With all their power the Japs would say, "We will," and with all we had we'd say, "You won't."

For our crew and the Big Moose, the big operation began in mid-July 1943. Besides bombing strikes, we also flew numerous 800 mile reconnaissance patrols over the open seas, antishipping skip bombing patrols, and searches for lost crews. We also guided fighters for long over-water flights, and carried supplies to distant places when needed.

At all times, the Big Moose never complained and never failed. It was a gentle 60,000 pounder that seemed to have a soul of its own. It hurt when we hurt. There were hundreds of B24s around, but this one was ours. When it returned from a mission full of holes, we felt the hurt. We would tell the crew chief to fix her up gently.

Air warfare, land warfare, and sea warfare each had its unique horrors. We did our war where a man cannot walk, breathe, hide, or live without support systems. The sky, five miles up, objected vigorously to man's presence with freezing temperatures and lack of air. It was difficult for Big Moose to stay in the thin atmosphere. When all systems in the airplane functioned, it grudgingly allowed us to stay up there. The least malfunction would send us downward.

It is ironic how we humans, in times of peace, putter around on the ground near our homes, raise flowers, go fishing, and date girls. When it comes to war, we trundle to the most remote areas (often the opposite side of the globe), sail into the deepest and widest oceans, climb to the highest limits of the atmosphere, and fight each other to the death. Those who survive go back home to grow flowers, make homes, and raise families.

Most crew members, except navigators who had a somewhat better world concept, asked, "Where in the hell are we?" Even though this navigator had never heard of Guadalcanal, the Solomon Islands, or the Admiralties; this is where his crew and Big Moose started the war.

The task of the Air Corps was to deny the Japs the supplies and facilities from which they could pursue their designs. Every second or third day, we raided Jap facilities on New Georgia, Munda, Vila, and Treasury Islands, and air bases at Kahili, Buin, Ballale and Buka on Bouganville. Also, we skip-bombed whatever shipping we found. Between raids, one or two days of respite were allowed to relieve fatigue and emotional tension. After about six raids, we lost our tail gunner through a nervous breakdown. He couldn't control his muscles nor see properly. We quickly received a replacement.

Each raid had its own characteristic set of horrors. In the high headquarters, the war was statistics, logistics, and politics. In the squadrons and individual airplanes, it was men and blood.

Between raids, we were unnerved by the empty bunks that had held our buddies the night before. We sorrowed for them, gathered up their belongings, and sent them home. Each episode like this diminished something within us.

Once we gathered around our airplane commander to spill our woes. "How long will this go on?" we asked. "We won't be able to take this much longer." I added a concern about being killed.

In his calmest and most soothing manner, the pilot rose to the occasion. He eased our fears, and made us feel we had a great chance to live through the fight. All we had to do was to survive 25 missions. After that, we had a good chance to go back to the U.S. He was an excellent pilot which added confidence to his assurance.

The Army Air Corps had a policy and a plan to maintain morale in the forward units. Bunks that became vacant were quickly filled. Increasing numbers of empty bunks, looked at night after night, were definitely morale busters.

After six weeks of combat flying, the whole squadron was allowed to move to a quiet rear area for rest. This lasted nearly three weeks. Nine of these days were spent in New Zealand.

This little fringe benefit was not available to ground crews. They labored without relief for the duration in all sorts of remote outposts. They experienced their own strains and tensions, and longed for diversion.

When combat crews were about to leave, ground crew members begged us to bring back whiskey. They offered to pay fantastic prices which, if accepted, bordered on outright theft. Such was the suffering of our wonderful maintenance men.

In New Zealand we rested, dated ladies, danced, were robbed by civilians, and ate fresh meat. We were rationed free whiskey at the rate of a fifth and a pint every five days.

Four of us commissioned members were given a well-furnished room at a very low price. Three of us were nondrinkers, but the bombardier was an alcoholic who would be continuously drunk if money and booze were amply available. The three of us drank up our allotment so the bombardier couldn't drink it.

It was when drinking that our long-dormant wisdom slowly emerged. We would converse about all sorts of disconnected topics with an abundance of profoundness.

"Oh, God smiles on the just and the unjust."

"Will the Japs who might shoot us down meet us in heaven?"

"Well, if the just and unjust are smiled upon — we surely will meet them."

"But how will we know which one did it?"

"St. Peter will introduce us and will tell us who did it."

"Hey. I don't think he should make me leave this earth yet! I'm a virgin!"

"Oh hell! That shouldn't make any difference."

"It should. Before I go I want to leave behind a bunch of kids."

"Yes, dying a virgin is a disaster."

"Hey boy! While I'm still a virgin, we'd better fly high and fast so we get back!"

"Shit, I'm no virgin. Gimme another drink you bastard. It's your fault if you're a virgin."

"Listen you turd, you can't talk like that."

"Treat women rough. They like it. Spread the white race all over the world."

"I didn't know you were such a shit!"

"You don't hear me bitching over what you are bitching about. Pass the bottle, dammit!"

"Listen you guys. Not many months ago I bailed out of an airplane. I was pushed by the terror that I hadn't accomplished anything yet. What's really important is whether you leave the world a better place than you found it, not the status of your virginity."

"Listen to that philosophic blurb."

"Now listen to me, bub. Any damn fool can devirginize himself at any time. To accomplish something worthwhile and lasting takes a man who is worth something."

"We won't fight the Japs too well if we fight each other."

"Where do you think the war is taking us?"

"I don't know. We only have a worm's eye view of the real world even though we do fly high. Like a poet said, 'Ours is not to reason why; ours is but to do and die'."

"How we are blasting hell out of those bastards! And they are bashing us, and punching holes in our Big Moose. God must be watching this. Is he happy? Isn't it hard to believe that a world committing suicide is a creation of a supreme and benevolent intelligence."

"What you ask has been pondered for ages. How can we poor muzhiks answer this here and now? Maybe we all need another drink. It might loosen more hidden wisdom from our craniums. Let's drink. Ah! One group thinks they have an answer. Another group thinks they have the answer. They then get together and argue with great fervor. Finally, they began killing each other."

"I hate to think that in the event of my demise, I'd leave nothing good and lasting. It would be like dropping a pebble in a pool, a few waves for a short while, and a still pool again as if the pebble had never dropped. I'd like to blast a hole in granite so it would be seen for centuries. Devirginizing yourself, something we just argued about, is as lasting as a fart."

"Damn, but I'm getting sleepy. We came up here to let off steam, rejuvenate ourselves. We haven't felt feminine skin for months. I've forgotten what the opposite sex smells like."

"Here we are, trying to drown our woes with this damn booze. We are forgeting that feminine companionship is the best rejuvenator of all."

"Yeh, after philosophizing our time away we'll still have that war to fight. Let us charge into the world of softness, fragrance, tenderness, and beauty. To hell with the war."

"Boy but I'm sleepy, I'm going to z-z-z-z-z for a while."

And z-z-z-z it was for the rest of the day and all night.

The bottles had very little contents.

The remainder of our stay in New Zealand was spent rejuvenating. The Red Cross sponsored enjoyable dances and entertainment.

We rented an automobile and drove all over the countryside on the wrong side of the road. Car rental required a $50 deposit, plus a set fee per day. Theoretically, the initial deposit was to be refunded upon return of the auto. However, rental agencies usually found so much wrong with returned cars that seldom was any money refunded. Having to leave the country left no time to protest, and the troops were in no mood for any more fighting, even if time were available.

By the ninth day, according to the Air Corps, the men should be rejuvenated and anxious to fight. The pilot had kept daily contact with crew members, gave pep talks, and looked after their welfare.

A C47 transport was ready to fly us to Guadalcanal. Just before boarding, our pilot collapsed. We were told it was a nervous breakdown. We flew back a pilotless crew.

The flight surgeon explained that our pilot had forced upon himself a calm manner. While showing an outward calmness, he was experiencing internal turmoil which he worked hard to hide. We were assured that his condition was temporary and that shortly he would rejoin the crew.

Upon landing on Guadalcanal, someone came up and hollered "Which one of you guys is Maleckas?"

"I am," I said.

"You are flying tomorrow morning—early. Report to operations as soon as you can."

"I can't fly tomorrow," I said. "Our crew has no pilot."

"I know that," he said. "I am to tell you that you're flying tomorrow and to report to operations immediately."

"OK sergeant," and off I went.

*Aldon A. Alleman, my first pilot. He had well developed plans to manufacture helicopters after the war. We lost him in a storm near White City, Kansas, January 5, 1943.*

It turned out that on a previous mission, a crew's navigator had been shot and was in bad condition. I was to substitute until our own pilot returned. "OK," I said, and began the usual preparations.

This was to be mission number 16 for me, if only bomb drop missions were counted. It was number 18 if flights where fire was exchanged with the Japanese reconnaissance planes was counted. Twenty-four if skip-bombing and submarine patrol missions were counted. In skip-bombing and submarine searches, we had no opportunity to use weapons so they probably were not considered strikes.

At squadron operations, the planes and crews were already posted on a long chalkboard. Every position had a man assigned by name and rank. Ours was to carry an eleventh man, a bombardier, who was to observe and become oriented to combat operations.

I sought out the plane commander and introduced myself. He happened to be a fellow I had seen around the squadron. I knew little of him except that he had had more than his share of bad luck on missions. Besides losing a navigator, he had lost several other-crew members on previous raids. He was easy to talk to, and we talked at length about many things, but he avoided discussion about his combat missions.

He was from Chicago. Like myself, he was the son of an immigrant. He was to be married as soon as he got home. Finally, he said, "It is late and we must rise early. Let's hit the sack."

# Chapter 4

It was a long day. In the morning I was in New Zealand, a colorful place with bright lights, people dressed in a variety-of apparel, restaurants with fresh eggs and meat, night clubs with ladies and music and booze, newsstands with magazines and papers, automobiles with civilians, streets lit up with lamps, tall buildings with lots of glass windows. The skys were empty of roaring behemouths, no explosions or air raid sirens were heard, and no shrill whistles jarred one out of bed in the pitch dark morning.

Now, I found myself suddenly in a world not merely at zero, but below zero by a good measure. Entering the long, squat, dark, and steamy hut a thought came drilling into my cerebellum. What kind of world is the real one?

A kind of scornful feeling oozed through my being about the world I had just come from. I had been in the Army over two years, every day of which was spent in pursuit of some grim deed or in preparation for it.

It was a serious world wherein a failure or misdeed meant some degree of tragedy. Somewhere, somehow, something would get you. You could end up with a nasty job, lose prestige or self esteem, lose the love of your girl friend, lose a promotion, lose your life at a young age. You might even find yourself permanently horizontal and out of sight.

You had to be continually swimming upstream against a

strong current. You either had to be going ahead, or you went backward.

There were no flowers to smell, no time to listen to the birds, no paintings to admire, no soft skin to touch, no perfumed fragrance to enjoy, no lips to kiss, and no time to stand and stare. There were only great machines, smoke, smashing and crashing, brutality, pushing the human body to its limits, vast statistics to build up, blood, fear, and grimness.

This was the world, the real world as it was meant to be. The world I had just come from had not come to grips with reality. It was a dream world, a trite world, steeped in superfluities, living in and choosing illusions. They think the world is all sweetness, soft beds, and cool rooms, green grass, and flowers. They don't know what's going on.

Having so reflected, I shuffled to my cot. Most of the men had already retired, with a few conversing in hushed tones. This was the night before a mission for these men. You could tell by their slumber. Men who had a strong propensity to snore slept silently the night before a mission.

Forty men, tossing and trembling in their crosslegged cots, produced squeaks in a variety of pitches. Some poor soul would eventually sink into slumber only to plunge into a nightmare, whereupon his nearby buddy would awaken him.

Before most missions the wakeup whistle blew between four and five o'clock. It took at least 10 hours to wake, clean up, eat, be briefed, board the airplane, warm up, wait for take off, take off, assemble into squadrons and groups, rendezvous with fighters, fly to target, drop, return, fly the landing pattern, land, and debrief the mission.

On October 25, 1943, I awoke at four, a half-hour before

the whistle. I had a lot of mail to read. It was my younger sister's eighth birthday and I planned to write to her when I returned.

I gathered all the letters from my girlfriend. They conveyed warmth and love and described how proud she was of her pickle crop last summer. It was a good crop.

Momentarily, I lapsed into a fantasy world and basked in the sweetness and love her words carried to me. How much easier it was to go on doing this thing after hearing one loving word.

There was a letter from the mother of my first pilot, full of the same love and concern that she had lavished on her own son.

A letter from Mom and Dad tried to hide sorrow and worry between every line. Dad, tough muzhik that he was, hardened by conflict, still had a soft heart and tender feelings. With me away and other young people in the area in the armed forces, there was little outside help to run the farm. Mom assumed the role of a man and worked the fields with Dad.

Dad's words of caution were, "Take care of yourself and be careful. Don't fly high. Fly low and slow where it is safe."

While absorbed in private reverie, a couple of my own crew came in, sad eyed and bowed. "Sir," said one, "did you know that while we were away the Big Moose was lost?" The shock jarred me. It was as though we'd lost some dear friend. "Really?" I said, "I didn't know. What the hell else is going to happen?" We stood and stared into each others eyes, trying to detect a tear while trying to hide our own.

"What'll we do now sir?" they asked. How could I answer? Desperately I thought of some memorial-tribute but only said, "Let's wait for our pilot to come back. We'll talk about it then and think of something."

The men left. I said, "Damn it all to hell, has the world gone berserk?" The Big Moose was gone. How much affection we lavished on that machine. How badly we felt when we found it full of holes and damaged parts after a mission! How we conferred with the crew chief about the repairs and treatment to be expended on this airplane.

I thought about how I had listened for hours to the hum of its engines across the full width of the Pacific. How dependable they sounded and how they seemed to have a soul that was concerned about our safety and welfare. They seemed to have promised to carry us back across the Pacific.

When other crews flew the Moose, we would query about its condition after they returned. Now, it was gone.

I wanted to cry but didn't. Men didn't cry about anything in this business. Uncommon tragedies were common. They grieved inwardly in cold silence for lost buddies with no sign of hatred toward adversaries. They went at their tasks without hesitation or outward show of fear. Orders came, missions were performed, losses were endured, and silent grief was suffered as we rested and waited for the next orders. The great war machine ground ceaselessly and resolutely on; never failing to produce all sorts of debris along the way.

In the squadron briefing room, the commander gave a short summary of the day's situation.

The Army and Marines were about to make major moves in the western Solomons, the nature of which was not made clear. Several sweeps by B25s would be made soon after our drop. Then the fighters would strafe. The whole object of this operation was to neutralize the Jap's air and "keep their heads down" as he put it.

The flight leader assigned the positions of each aircraft,

and specified rates of climb and attack altitudes. Ours was the right side of the lead element of three planes. We would assume the lead position should the original lead plane fall out for any reason.

The lead bombardier described types of bombs, fuse settings, bomb spacing, drop altitudes, aiming points, and such technicalities particular to his speciality.

The lead navigator outlined the route to and from the target.

Finally, the weather officer and the intelligence officer made their input.

Instructions outlined what to do in case of crashing enroute, over target, and on return. Since the route was more than 90% over deep water and out of sight of land, these instructions were not very reasssuring. Should we be fortunate enough to bail out over land, it was suggested that we avoid being shot down over Bouganville for the Japs there were hostile and the natives were not to be trusted. However, we were told that on Choiseul the natives were friendly and that we should choose to crash there. This bit of humor brought some grins.

A hundred men stoically listened, took notes concerning their particular function, made time hacks, fidgeted in their seats, and talked little. Most had been through this ritual many times.

At this time, the goal of all crews was to succeed in doing 25 missions. After that, members become eligible for consideration to return to the U.S.; provided there were replacements and no hitches.

As the conflict wore on, the men began to look on their jobs as though they were delivering coal to someone who didn't care to have it. The attitude was, "Let's hurry up and get this over with so I can go home. I have this and that to do."

Waiting trucks took us to our widely dispersed bombers. Then we began a process of positioning for takeoff. Each plane had a definite assigned place.

At a given signal, the huge bombers began to roar down the runway at 50-second intervals, each using the full length of the runway before airborne.

Today, we carried a maximum load of 1,000-pound bombs and 50 caliber ammunition. We were on our way as the sun began to show in the east.

Dressing for high altitude operations in this part of the world was tricky. On the ground the temperature ranged between 80 and 95 steamy degrees Fahrenheit. At attack altitudes (which usually varied from 20,000 to 24,000 feet) the temperature was between 40 and 50 degrees below zero Fahrenheit.

We learned to add clothing as we climbed, ending with the parachute harness and a "Mae West." Once fully dressed, I was so bulky that there was very little room for movement in the tight compartment.

For some reason, the rookie bombardier chose to observe from my compartment behind the pilots. Also, the top gunner turret swung in my compartment. In an emergency, I thought it would be useless to try to get out.

I didn't like this but I didn't say anything. I squeezed into my corner and began to monitor and log altitude, course, speed, temperature, and position. Should it be necessary to abort the mission, we would need to know where we were and where to go.

I looked out the small window to the left of my desk. I saw the leader, slightly above and ahead in a gentle climb. The engines labored as never before to lift our maximum load.

I loved the sound of those engines and thought of the Big Moose and how it rested somewhere in the "big deep."

The planes bobbed gently up and down relative to each other. It gave a sensation of being fixed in space with no speed.

I prayed that the lead plane would fly the mission to conclusion. Otherwise, ours would have to take the front position.

At 8,000 feet we went on oxygen until we descended to that altitude sometime after the drop. I stood to check the pilots. They were tense, gripping the wheel very hard with one hand and the throttles with the other.

Far out at sea and at the attack altitude of 23,000 feet, we made a turn to a southwesterly course toward the initial point on Bouganville. Below, storm clouds covered the ocean. Ahead loomed huge vertical cumulus clouds rising to about 35,000 feet. We would have to fly around them and proceeded to do so. The gunners were testing their guns. Each reported to the pilot he was ready, and tension began to mount. The temperature read 40 degrees below, and my toes were freezing.

Suddenly, the pilot called, "Pilot to crew. Look sharp, I spot bogies at one o'clock and eleven o'clock."

Six gunners reported, "Roger."

From my small window I could not see them. The formation began making sharp turns to avoid vertical cloud developments.

The top turret swung and fired a long burst. Hot, spent shell casings poured down into my compartment.

The rookie bombardier wedged himself between the pilots to avoid the swinging turret, thus blocking what little view I had.

Except for the small window, it felt like I was in a submarine.

Other gunners began to fire and vibrate the plane. Then came a sound like a huge chain slapped against the side of the plane in the bomb bay area. At the same time an enormous G-force slammed my face onto the navigation table, causing my nose to bleed into the oxygen mask.

The rookie bombardier collapsed to the floor and the turret gunner came crashing out of his turrent on top of him. I had no chance to ascertain what had happened. I was in the process of buckling on my chest chute when this began and had yet to snap on the lower straps.

The plane began whipping and spinning causing the three of us to smash against one wall, then the other. I struck my head on something which caused sparks in my eyes and blurred my vision.

There wasn't much time to think anything except, "This is the end . . . definitely no chance. How will it feel to have life extracted from my body? Where will the life go?" I relaxed to allow the inevitable to happen.

On other occasions, I had watched B24s plummet to earth from great heights and wondered what went through the minds of the people inside. I was about to learn.

I cringed and tightened every muscle, waiting for the impact. Nothing occurred. I felt myself saying, "Dammit - hurry up."

The motors screamed like I had never heard them before. The whipping and spinning was extraordinarily violent. It felt as if the airplane had broken apart.

Between the bomb bay and navigator's compartment was a bulkhead with a spring-loaded door that slipped upward when a latch was pressed. During our thrashing around, the latch was somehow struck and the bulkhead door opened. I saw a way to get out.

I waited for a tumble that would take me past the door. By seizing the edge of the opening and partially aided by centrifugal force, I flung myself into cold space.

The whole rear half of the plane behind the wing was

missing. The wings with all four motors in full power and the nose section with my compartment instantly disappeared into the clouds below.

Extreme silence enveloped me. A short minute ago I was amid a fleet of roaring bombers. Now, I was surrounded by a painful silence, with no sound from the formation and only a frigid wind rushing past my face.

Quickly the realization that I was falling hit me. Below was a thick undercast which made me estimate that I was about 15,000 feet up and that I had already fallen about 10,000 feet. It was bitter cold as I fell without benefit of oxygen.

I took deep breaths but little air came in. "If I'm going to pass out," I thought, "I'd better open the chute."

With great effort, I lifted one arm which seemed to weigh a hundred pounds, grasped the ring and pulled. I didn't have the strength to pull it out.

Through the clouds I plunged. I began to feel warmer air and my lungs were filling up with oxygen. Strength returned to my arms. I pulled the rip cord to open the chute.

My fall was abruptly slowed by a sharp jerk on my armpits. I realized I hadn't buckled the chute harness under my legs. If I relaxed my arms, I would fall out.

I placed the palms of my hands against my head which kept the straps from slipping past my elbows. Thus I floated down into the warmer air below the overcast.

At what I thought was 30 feet above water, I relaxed my arms and fell out of the chute into the ocean. The wind picked up the chute and carried it out of sight.

A tinge of sadness crept through me to discard that beautiful, gleaming white, round thing that had saved my life. I looked to see what time it was. My watch had been lost. It was probably eleven o'clock in the morning.

When the air bubble caught in my clothing leaked out, I began to sink. I remembered the Mae West and inflated it. Then came a shock. This life preserver on which we showered so much affection was not a life preserver, but a corpse preserver. If one drowned it would keep the body afloat.

It puffed out into a big bulge over my chest which caused me to roll over in the water with my body underneath it and my face under the surface. It was like taking a balloon into the ocean and trying to relax by staying on top of it. To save oneself with this life preserver, one had to swim like hell or drown.

My shoes felt like rocks tied to my feet. I struggled to discard them, saving the laces which I tied around my neck. I kept discarding clothing until I came to the flight overalls and winter underwear. These I decided to live with come what may.

In the hazy distance to the south, about 15 miles away I could see the island of Choiseul. If I should ever reach it, I would need protection from mosquitoes.

A heavy 45 caliber pistol with three clips of ammunition hung around my neck. It tended to pull me down and was difficult to swim with. Should I discard it? I conducted an internal debate.

Should I make Choiseul, I would find it infested with Japs who took no prisoners and never surrendered themselves. I would make every effort to hide, but if cornered I would not surrender. I would need this gun to shoot it out with them. So, swim or sink, I did not part with the pistol.

While undressing, I noted a lot of blood on my clothing, my face, and hands. Though I felt painful gouges all over my body, it didn't seem that so much blood much would have come from them.

*Somehow I managed to force my way out of the aircraft. When I was free, I pulled the rip cord. Then, I remembered I had forgotten to fasten my leg straps.*

My left leg just below the calf had a stinging pain, but underwater I couldn't do anything to it.

With preliminary preparations for survival completed, I began to look around and decide what to do.

It was extremely lonely. At all briefings I began to recall we were instructed that if forced to crash in the big deep we were to stay in place. The position would be reported by surviving crews and a PT boat or seaplane would rescue me.

With that thought, I decided to stop worrying and begin waiting. About four hours from now the bombers would all be home. During debriefing my position would be reported and maybe a seaplane would arrive before sundown. Until then I'd have to fight to stay afloat with this damned "Mae West." It was the most worthless piece of junk we ever depended on. It was going to be a constant fight to stay above water.

I felt the skin on my face. It was covered with oil. In fact, my whole body was sticky with oil. "Ah, the bomber must have crashed on this very spot," I thought. "Maybe there are survivors around here."

There was no sign of life, but soon I began to spot big yellow oxygen bottles. They were bobbing in the oil all around me. There were about a dozen close by.

I gathered them with the idea of making a raft by tying them together. With only two shoe strings, I was able to tie only three of them together by connecting the spouts on each end. Hanging on to them considerably reduced the struggle to stay afloat and alive.

In about an hour I saw a beautiful and a joyous sight. A single B24 returning from a raid came flying low and slowly began circling my position. I gathered as many oxygen bottles around me and splashed water as hard as I could. They spotted me.

On the first pass over they took a good look. A waist gunner waved and I waved back. I thought they were trying to ascertain if it was truly a B24 survivor and not a Jap fighter pilot.

On the second pass, they dropped a life raft which landed about three feet from me. What a joyous sight!

In a few seconds, however, it became a heartbreak. The dropper forgot to pull the inflation cord when he tossed it out. The raft sank. The crew, low on fuel and thinking they had accomplished a great rescue, flew home. I was left hanging on to the improvised raft, wet and in tears.

I never met the crew that made this gallant effort to

make my lot easy. Forty years later, my son-in-law was conversing with a fellow worker about things past. This led to the latter's discussion of his war experiences. He described an incident wherein he dropped a life raft from a B24 to a man in the water.

My son-in-law who had heard my story about the tragedy, became alert and began to question for details. Comparing the two stories as to dates, times, and places, it turned out that this fellow did indeed drop the raft. He did not remember pulling the inflation knobs and to this day did not know that it had sunk.

I went to visit him and found that he kept a diary. It contained all the details to confirm this episode.

★★★

From the sun, I calculated that it was about an hour past noon or thereabouts. I felt the rescue would surely come not 1ater than noon the next day. On a number of occasions, our crew participated in rescue searches for downed crews; our bomber loaded with inflatable rafts, food, and water. The Army Air Corps never gave up on lost people until every effort was made to find them. I felt good about taking part, and now I felt good knowing that the same would be done for me. There remained only the wait.

Hours began to pass. The longest hours one could possibly experience. I clung to the oxygen-tank raft. Whatever told me to save those strings when I discarded the shoes? It made such a difference now. Without them, I would have had to fight to stay atop the life preserver or cling to some slippery oxygen bottle. Most likely, I would have succumbed to exhaustion.

Now, I simply hung on to the strings, legs and body

hanging straight down and water halfway up my chin.

The Mae West, in time, became flat and useless. It had been punctured.

I began to notice sea life all around. Large schools of fish would simultaneously jump out of the water and go back with a loud splash. Some were very close. Something must have been chasing them.

I began to worry about swordfish and wondered what they used their swords for. And sharks. Life rafts carried shark repellent among other things for survival. I had none. In fact, I had no survival items except the gun.

I had been very survival conscious to the extent that some made humorous comments. I carried double of most items required to survive in water or jungle. Instead of one first aid kit, I carried two. One in a canvas belt next to my skin and the other in a rifleman's ammunition belt. Instead of one quart of fresh water, I carried two. The ammo belt carried fishhooks and lines, concentrated chocolate bars, sardines, knife, matches, flashlight, and a jack knife. Under the seat, I also kept a hatchet.

It was a lot of trouble lugging these on every mission, and created problems in the limited space. I was hungry and thirsty, but was without the things I struggled to have along on flights. During the tumbles, they must have snagged on something in the plane.

I scanned the waters around hoping to see the other crew members. I yelled with hopes of an answer. If they couldn't see, maybe they could hear. I was alone for sure. Far to the south a faint outline of a mountain showed on Choiseul. Oh, it looked far!

Besides the tinkling of the waves, it was extremely quiet. The dark outline of some large sea creature approached and remained motionless a few feet from me. A shark I thought. "Well, here's where I join the other members of the crew," I said to myself. I waited. It simply disappeared. Several times these things came to examine me only to go away. There was time; long, long, hours to think, think, think.

After what seemed like several months, the sun reached the horizon. Looking around I spotted a small life raft. It was floating low in the water. It had a long rip across the bottom. I climbed into it.

Even with the rip, it still was able to keep an air bubble at each end. I figured if I lay real still, the air would not be forced out the tear and I would be able to rest horizontally with my feet and head dry and the middle submerged. For the first time, I could relax. I released two oxygen bottles, saved the string, and tethered the other bottle onto the raft. Night descended.

The wind shifted direction, seemed a bit stronger, and was blowing toward Choiseul. I lay as motionless as possible to save what little air I had in the raft. Above the sound of waves, I could hear sea life splashing around. A big surprise was the spark-like flashes that sea water produced when disturbed. I was able to turn my head around and look down into the deep and see a trail of sparks made by a speeding fish or something.

My butt protruded through the tear in the raft into the water. Fish, or something else, would bump or nibble at it all night long. However, none made a serious bite. Somewhere underneath me, maybe a hundred feet or a thousand or even fifty, were ten crew members. Even the Big Moose might be resting close by.

The Big Moose, was a good airplane. How it took punishment without complaint, lifted tremendous loads, responded willingly to controls, and flew vast distances to bring us safely home. Somebody had to destroy it and the men.

I imagined the wires humming across the Pacific taking messages to the families of the men on my crew and their families' reactions. All would be similar to that of the parents of a bombardier whose body I had escorted home after an accident.

Nowhere in literature had I read a description of the grief and sorrow that kin undergo because of the loss of a loved one. There are great stories of battles and victories with heroes dashing forth to their rewards. Nowhere has attention been given to ones who have fallen, whose blood was seeping out and life slowly ebbing away. No one has ever paid attention to these fellows, their thoughts, their feelings, or their wishes.

I knew that shortly Mom and Dad would be receiving a message of my predicament. They would receive a "missing in action" message. All their lives they received small rewards from their great labors. I could not see fit to shed tears for my situation, but fought to hold in tears at the thought of the grief and sorrow they would have to endure. There were my two sisters. I'd seen so little of them since high school. I was sorry.

Einstein is known to have said, "To sit on a hot stove for a minute seems like an hour." Here, waiting for the night to pass, each hour seemed endless. Sleep was not possible, for however still I tried to lay in the raft, the wave action caused the air in the bubble to seep out little by little. Just like the puncture that produced a flat Mae West.

I judged the time of night by watching stars, a fringe benefit that navigators had over others.

Toward morning, I looked toward the island of Choiseul. The wind and the tide had carried me very close, probably within a mile. This created another worry. I would not be in the reported position for the sea plane when it came for me in the morning. Also, it probably would not venture too close to the island, for it was Jap occupied and dangerous. Though I had kept my life simple, everything that had happened conspired to make things difficult. "What the hell's the use of trying," I began to think. Maybe by surviving I had cheated some power that was gleefully watching while slowly trying to do me in.

By sunup, I began to notice that the distance to the island had increased. I felt better, thinking that rescue planes were taking off at this very instant and that it would be easier to find me closer to the reported position. We always took off at sunrise for rescue missions.

I relaxed and felt secure, though the raft would barely hold me up. By noon it would sink and I'd be alone with one oxygen bottle and the Mae West. I noticed that the bottle had taken on water through the end outlet and was low in the water. I removed the water by blowing into one end and expelling it out the other. I also reinflated the chest preserver by blowing into the inflation tubes.

By midmorning, the raft seemed to give up. I tied the ends of a shoestring to each end of the bottle making a hand hold. Morning turned to noon, and there was no sound of rescue. Only silence, silence, silence. I was drifting further and further out to sea. By mid-afternoon I became certain that no one was going to come out.

"Damn those sons-of-bitches!" I exclaimed. "What the hell is keeping them? I worked my butt off looking for others. Now no one is looking for me."

By this time I hadn't eaten, drunk, or slept for 35 hours. I decided to swim to the island. It seemed about five miles away. An almost impossible distance for one in my condition. It would take effort and time.

My mind flashed back to Dad. "Time and effort were

the cheapest and most abundant commodities that one possessed," he'd say. He scorned anybody who recoiled from a task because it would take too much time or effort. He did not take into account how much time it took to accomplish something. He just went and did it. He would work just as long and as hard for a nickel as he would for a dollar.

One who did not work and produce however little, was worthless in his book. He classified as worthless kings, queens, all manner of royalty, bosses, loafers, and lawyers. He ranked lawyers especially low since he once had to pay a month's pay for a half-an-hour of a lawyer's time. Mother went along with Dad in this philosophy. If you didn't work, you had no excuse for existing. So I reflected on what Dad or Mom would do in this situation. They would swim. Dammit, so would I. There were Japs, but to hell with them.

From then until sundown, I swam pushing the oxygen bottle ahead and struggling to keep the life preserver under. I could not tell if I was making headway, which tended to be discouraging. At sundown, the oxygen bottle was full of water and sank. I salvaged the shoe string and wrapped it around my neck. The gun and ammo became heavier and heavier. Eventually, pitch darkness came.

It was now over 40 hours since I'd had sleep, drink, or food. Midnight came and went, the Mae West and the gun added to my misery.

The island was much closer, and I was encouraged knowing I was making progress. I believed the tide was helping. I could hear the waves breaking against the shore.

A bright glow outlined the island, and I heard band music. A huge door opened on the side of the cliff revealing a bright interior, and a white submarine came out. There was a line of street lights along the shore with traffic on a highway.

My arms and legs were becoming numb and immobile from exhaustion. I debated with myself. What will be the reward for my efforts? My folks would have settled for zero for their efforts, but I was facing a big minus. Besides, I'd exhausted all available effort. Nobody would blame me if I quit and drowned myself.

I heard harp music. It came from what appeared to be glowing angels with wings flapping on their ankles and harps in their hands. There were about six of them dancing in a circle around me and singing.

I felt I had to speak to them. I asked them what I should do. They replied together, "Do whatever you feel you should do. We'll be with you whatever you do." I said, "I'm exhausted and I've decided to drown. The Japs will do me in if I get ashore."

They replied, "Whatever you do, we'll be with you."

I said, "You're not helping me. What should I do?"

"We cannot decide for you. We can only be with you no matter what you decide," they said.

I said, "I can't move any more."

They said, "We will not leave you."

I relaxed with the thought of inhaling the deepest possible breath of water into my lungs. My feet went down. At armpit deep, my feet hit bottom and I stood.

It was about 45 hours since my feet last touched the soil on Guadalcanal. I stood and rested. The eastern horizon was showing signs of the rising sun. Strength began to return to my arms and legs. The glow about the island disappeared, as did the street lamps, the traffic, and the submarine door in the cliff. The six glowing angels flew away, and the sound of breakers against the shore became loud.

I threw away the Mae West and swam about 300 yards to shore. I landed at the foot of a 30 foot cliff strewn with sharp coral rocks. I had to climb out of the water. My first impulse was to run as fast and as far into the jungle as possible. The Japs would find me if I didn't.

Unfortunately, my legs were like cooked noodles and the urge to sleep was too great. I climbed onto a coral rock. With its sharp projections cutting into my body, I fell asleep.

I found this poem in our bomb group's operations room sometime in July 1943. These poignant words had a sobering effect when we had losses.

★ ★ ★ ★

### "One Plane Did Not Return"

*Oh God! The crippled wings ceased their flying.*
*And I am setting out alone on death's dark sea...*
*I who loved life, with ne'er a thought of dying,*
*My blood exultant, death so far from me!*
*Who thrilled warm to a girl's sweet laughter,*
*Shouted and sung in my young manhood's pride,*
*Bent to the oar and cleft the sunlit water,*
*Breasted the wave and fought the running tide!*
*Grant this my prayer: Doom not the after years*
*Of men to war...and all the bitter price*
*Of young love unfulfilled, and the sad tears*
*Be worthless, nor in vain my sacrifice.*
*Make my last failing breath a trumpet voice:*
*"Ever in peace may every land rejoice!"*

–Thomas Carlyle Adamson-(6-2-43)
Pocket Book Wireless Weekly, March 6, 1943

★ ★ ★ ★

These words echoed through my whole being when I found myself in deep water and the grim reaper never far away.

# Chapter 5

In time, I awoke and looked about. I was draped over a coral boulder like a limp rag. Projections from the rock were poking into my belly and ribs. I was beginning to hurt. I guessed I had hurt all along, but only now did I begin to feel it.

The tide was out; much of the coral fragment covered sand was exposed. I vaguely recalled that when I came ashore the rock I was on was partially submerged by the sea. It must have been high tide. A vertical, 40-foot cliff sloped downward for about 100 yards along the beach westward and disappeared in jungle growth eastward.

I decided to climb off the rock and trundle up the beach and see what was what. Sliding down, I collapsed like an overcooked length of spaghetti. Every muscle hurt and protested demands made on it. I was very weak. I lay there awhile and thought.

I had no idea of the hour, day, or month. The sun was either three hours after sunrise or three hours before sunset. After some minutes, my mind began to clear and I ascertained that the sun was westward and day was ending. I had lain in the hot sun all day. My face and hands were severely sunburned.

It felt comfortable to lie in the warm sand even though my burned skin throbbed in pain. I wanted to stretch out and go to sleep. How good it felt to be straight and level again and not to have to move.

Thoughts began to seep into my cranium; events of the recent past, the explosion, the night in the water, the long swim, the fate of the crew, and the visions. The urge to fall asleep was great, but I remembered that the spot I was lying on was in deep water when I first came. I couldn't stand up and walk. On hands and knees, I crawled along the sand until the cliff receded and the beach gently sloped upward and joined the jungle. There in the soft sand I settled to sleep.

The ocean was calm and quiet. I thought about how rough it had been when I was in it. Every wave tended to submerge me making it difficult for me to swim. To hell with all you elements that made it difficult for me to save myself. Piss on you. I survived and am going to sleep. Try to do something now.

The birds screamed and screeched and their calls echoed through the still jungle. How peaceful and welcome they made me feel. For the first time since I'd left my country, I noticed the birds. They'd been around all the time. On Guadalcanal they sang, only to be drowned out by the constant roar of big engines. Besides, we were too concerned and occupied with what we had to do. Here, they were louder and more numerous than at home. Some seemed happy and some angry. I listened.

Just before slumber made its attack, something in the deep interior of my cranium sent a shock through my body. It had been three days since I had eaten or drank, but I was neither hungry nor thirsty. Two of those days were under maximum effort. Something was not adding up right. I had a great urge to sleep, but I'd just gotten up. Maybe this was actually the onset of unconsciousness from which I might not awaken. Another snare to do me in! I decided to eat and drink before going to sleep. No matter how much my muscles protested.

I noticed large numbers of small crabs scampering about the beach. They were timid but too quick for my slow action. I gave up on them and crawled into the jungle for greens. There I found dandelion-looking plants that tasted fair, buds of flowers, and the leaves, roots, and shoots of young plants. I ate them.

Soon, wonder of wonders, I found a puddle of fresh water with mosquito larvae wiggling in it. A source of meat, I thought. I drank and drank.

The crabs on the beach would make good nourishment, but how was I to catch them? After rummaging about in the bush, I found a stick that I could use to help me stand up and walk. On the beach, I was able to whack the crabs with it and stun them. Until the sun went down, I whacked and devoured crabs, dozens of them. Only the claws were good to eat and they weren't very big.

With my belly full of raw crabmeat, mosquitoes, weeds, and water, I felt safe to go to sleep with the hope that a rebellion would not develop in my digestive system. I listened to the commotion in my stomach and worried a little. Happily, it eventually subsided.

Just as I began to be embraced by comfort from the warm sand, swarms of mosquitoes came. If I allowed them freedom to do their thing, I'd need a transfusion by morning or die from loss of blood.

Very tired, in pain all over, and weak, I removed the flying coveralls. I was naked except for the pistol, ammunition, and first aid kit. My body looked a mess. I was covered with black bruises and scabs. I had a hole through the lower left calf.

I scooped a trench in the sand, settled into it, scraped sand back over my body, and placed the coveralls over the top of my head. This exposed a minimum of my anatomy to the insects.

The gods of slumber could be stalled no longer. I disengaged the safety lever on the pistol, put it on my chest and went to sleep. My final thought was, "This is half-assed survival, but better than none." Being half-assed was a very undesirable condition among GIs at that time, while half-vast was much better.

During the night, after hours of deep slumber, I awakened with my body protesting in pain. It wanted desperately to turn, twist, and change position, but packed in sand it couldn't. Finally I said, "To hell with the bugs! There can't be much night left. I'll get out of the sand, roll around, and cover myself with my overalls. Then, I will sleep on. Damn the insects." Faintly, I recalled from history an admiral saying something like that about torpedoes. I could take the same position about mosquitoes.

Next morning, I was forced awake by the sun cooking the sand around me, the steam under my coveralls, and screaming body functions demanding attention.

Up the stick I climbed until fully perpendicular. Without the support of the slender piece of weed, I wouldn't have been able to stand.

I inventoried the feelings in the digestive system. All systems were functioning under protest, but functioning. I found myself naked and without a fig leaf, so I donned my only garment.

What should I do? What can I do? I must find something better to eat. I must move eastward, westward, or into the jungle. Into the jungle was out of the question for it took too much energy. Eastward down the beach?

During the flights, I carefully studied all the islands with the thought about our best route should we have to bail out. Remembering that eastward were waterlogged swamps with the jungle covering the beach and even

# FOUR MOTORED BOMBER CRASHES IN KANSAS; 11 DIE

January 5 '43

## Burns Soon After Takeoff; 'Chute Saves One.

Topeka, Kas., Jan. 7 (AP).—Eleven crewmen were killed in the crash of a Topeka air base four motored bomber three miles west of White City, Kas., late yesterday.

Base officials said today one man, 2d Lt. Frank Maleckas, Custer, Mich., parachuted to safety before the plane fell into a cornfield and burned 20 minutes after leaving the home field.

Lt. L. E. Larson, public relations officer, announced the dead as:

**Flight Officer James G. Masters**, Wisemantown, Ky.

**First Lt. Robert Clyne**, Tuscon, Ariz.

**Second Lt. John Sedor**, Hammond, Ind

**Second Lt. Norman A. Kendall**, Ruston, La.

**Second Lt. Clifford A. Smallwood**, Toledo, O.

**Second Lt. Aldon A. Alleman**, Santa Ana, Cal.

**Second Lt. Joseph P. Hulder Jr.** Annandale, N. J.

**Pvt. Leonard McNabb**, Republic, Mo.

**Pvt. Gustave Dzingoski**, Camden, N. J

**Staff Sergt. Vernon O. Larson**, Rochelle, Ill.

**Staff Sergt. Thomas P. Merlino**, Los Angeles.

A board began investigating the accident.

- From The Ludington Daily News, 1943

# Lt. Maleckas Is Reported Missing

November 1, 1943

SCOTTVILLE — Lt. Frank Maleckas, only son of Mr. and Mrs. Frank Maleckas of Fern, has been reported missing in Southwest Pacific area, according to word received by his parents Wednesday.

Lt. Maleckas, a graduate of Custer high school in 1936, attended Western Michigan College of Education at Kalamazoo before entering the Army Air corps.

Besides his parents, he has two sisters, Ruth and Veronica.

His many friends will remember that Lt. Maleckas experienced a miraculous escape when he parachuted from a burning plane over Kansas several months ago, the only member of the plane's crew to be saved.

extending into the sea, I chose the westward trek.

But westward was where the Japs were. Japs!! This was the first time I was shocked into the awareness that I was in enemy territory. This was Choisuel, a neighbor of Bouganville. We were attacking these islands constantly. The Japs no doubt were mad as hell and in no mood to embrace anyone such as me. Besides, the word making the rounds was that they took "no prisoners."

Calmness soon settled over me. I would conduct one 11 millionth of the war on this island. There was no other choice but to be brave. I checked out the pistol. It was horribly rusted from soaking in salt water.

"Damn," I thought. After swimming with it around my neck, fighting its weight to pull me under, now in time of need would it be in condition to fire? It was so heavy that I could hardly take aim with it. It fired beautifully. What a lovely piece of iron. I kissed it. I was not ready to exhibit my bravery. I was too hungry, too weak, and in pain.

Leaning heavily on the walking stick, I began to trudge with great effort westward up the beach, worried that at the end of the island were Japs. I captured numerous beach crabs along the way, crushed their claws in my teeth, and sucked out the meat and juice.

I also found large snails and snail-like creatures attached to rocks. Smashing them with the pistol, I found a liberal portion of a slimy and ugly oyster-like mass. Only by closing my eyes was I able to swallow them. I didn't dare chew them. After having eaten my fill, I continued down the beach. I whacked crabs and tied their claws on the shoestrings around my neck. It gave me the appearance of an ancient, primitive tribesman wearing a necklace of small bones.

Exhaustion was never far behind and soon caught up.

There wasn't much joy in the stomach either. It was probably ten o'clock in the morning when I decided to find a safe place to rest for the remainder of the day.

I was lucky to find two large trees that had fallen across each other at the edge of the beach. I crawled in behind them and sat down with my back against the bank. Any Jap patrol would have to come up and look down to see me. Tracks would not give me away for there were many on the beach. It felt good not to move. It was pain's turn to make itself felt. Awareness of my predicament began to slowly seep into my thinking.

Looking around my enclosure, I saw a number of coconuts. At last, something more enjoyable to eat! Alas, it had been decreed that if one is to enjoy goodies a price must be paid. Coconuts are covered with a very tough husk. To eat the meat I first must crack the husk. A human, equipped as I was, was not capable. I felt like a caged monkey with a heap of bananas just out of reach.

All that I owned on this island was a pistol, three clips of ammunition, a first aid kit, two shoestrings and a flying coverall. I took aboard on the last flight and on every other flight more than enough survival items. They consisted of an extra first aid kit, knife, fishhooks and line, matches, flashlight, chocolates, canned meat, two quarts of water, rope, and a hatchet. I cussed them for their extra bulk and how they snagged on all sorts of projections in the small space in the bomber. Even after seeing how our craft were disabled in combat and what little chance crews had to survive, I still prepared for a picnic. Now in time of need, I had nothing except coconuts laughing at me.

I was determined to subdue a coconut. I bashed it against the tree trunk until soft, and then peeled with my fingers, fiber by fiber. It took most of the day, but I got to it and devoured it. The firmness of its meat made my mouth bleed. It also was full of fluid that I saved and drank. For the first time since takeoff I relaxed from contentment rather than fatigue. Until now, all the hurts and pains had lower priority for attention than the needs for rest and food. Now, every sore made itself known. Behind the knees and on my shoulders where the coveralls rubbed, the skin was worn through and was now scabbed over. Flexing these areas beyond a point caused the scabs to break and bleed. Numerous lacerations were beginning to show signs of infection.

In this steamy climate wounds became infected quickly, and needed prompt medical attention. Each crewmember was issued a first aid kit and instructions in its use. It contained the new wonder drug sulfanilamide. The kit contained two dozen of the white pills that looked like aspirin tablets. We had been instructed to pulverize enough to cover a wound, then eat two and wait for the medics. However, in emergencies and if no medics were available, we were to eat the remainder.

I liberally powdered all sores and swallowed what was left. In weeks to come this proved to be a wise treatment. Infection stopped.

I sat till sunset trying to think, but dozed off. Mosquitoes began to make their appearance and could not be ignored. I disrobed as the previous night, half-buried myself in the sand, covered up with the coveralls, and went to sleep. A few mosquitoes found their way under the cover and made a lot of noise. I decided to hell with the mosquitoes. I was going to sleep.

The morning sun sneaking in between the logs made a hot spot on my body that awakened me. Sand clung to my skin. I itched all over. The skin on my face and scalp, which had been badly sunburned during the swim and first day on the beach, began to peel off in large patches.

It had been at least a week since takeoff on the mission. My beard had made its strong appearance. The hair on my head was sandy and salt crusted, and every one had its own independent orientation. My cheeks were sunken and the belly wall receded way past the ribs.

I seized a coconut and bashed and peeled it for about two hours. Its juice was refreshing, but the solid part was painful to eat and caused a bloody mouth. Then I finished eating the crab claws that I carried on the shoestrings. I used them just in time, for in the heat they were about to spoil. I felt affection toward the shoestrings. Besides the gun and coveralls, they were all I owned.

Another day had to be faced. I sat on the logs and looked out at the sea. Not too far out in the deep rested ten strong young men. On the opposite side of the globe ten families were grieving along with my own. Thoughts went to my girlfriend, Helen. I longed for her presence, her touch, and her voice. An unfinished letter was at the base for her. Heavy, gloomy depression descended on me.

What kind of a god would write a script that directed events such that are now taking place? Short years ago I was pulling stumps from virgin sand. Now, I was on the opposite side of the world and in one hell of a situation.

Every effort to take care of myself was like rolling a boulder up hill, or pushing a long piece of cooked spaghetti. I could stand and walk only with the aid of a stick, but the scabs which were now dry and thick, broke from flexing and bled.

I decided to stay in place and do something to prepare the shelter against mosquitoes. With sticks and twigs, I would make a roof over my quarters and camouflage it somewhat. This would force the mosquitoes to hunt their way in and denied them a straight-in diving approach. It also provided a fair chance for a shoot out should that happen.

There was about 250 feet of beach from the edge of the jungle at low tide. Half of it was soft sand, and the rest quite firm from wetting by the tides. That's where I saw most of the footprints that I assumed were from Jap patrols.

I had to penetrate into the bush for materials. It was necessary to limit myself to twigs, branches, and broad leaves that I could break with my bare hands. Most of the damned vegetation had strong fiber and wouldn't separate after breaking. A knife would have made the job a pleasure. A human is almost useless without tools.

The most useful plant was the banana tree. It produced long, wide leaves that were ideal for top cover. There were abundant wild banana trees, but, damn it, no bananas. Yes, there were no bananas.

Fortune smiled a faint smile. I found puddles of water, which was fresh though muddy in taste, and a tree that produced nuts with a good supply fallen on the ground. The nuts resembled Brazil nuts but weren't, and they had a tough shell. By placing them on a log and whacking them with the gun, I opened them. Sometimes I had to strike hard and worried that the gun would fire. But it didn't. It took the abuse and was at all times ready to shoot. It was badly rusted but still performed. I loved it. It felt like a companion and made me feel not quite so lonely.

There were a few hours of daylight left, so I decided to sit on the shelter and feed the fatigue that began to seep in. I looked toward the ocean to the spot where I thought the aircraft went down. Gloom mixed with hopelessness began to claim my being. The thought of all those fellows not too far out in their deep watery grave filled my eyes with tears.

I made quick glances to the right and left to see if

anyone was watching, for soldiers weren't supposed to cry. When back at the base, we all experienced shock when crews failed to return. We felt deep sadness as we gathered up their personal effects, packaged them for shipment home, and cleaned the quarters for replacement crews. No one shed tears. It seemed that there was an unwritten rule that good soldiers never cried.

Thoughts drifted helter skelter over a wide spectrum of the human drama in crisis. Would I have been more comfortable if I had been a real religious person? Maybe. There must be a Great Script Writer somewhere that has the part for each of us written out and directs the course for human kind like an orchestra.

Does the Great Script Writer always write wisely? Why does he permit mothers to raise their children with joy, have them feel pride in their achievement, hope for their future, and then destroy them in a conflict not of their making? It seemed to me that the Great Script Writer enjoyed teasing his creation by first giving joy and then dousing it with great grief.

Maybe during his writings he was annoyed by mosquitoes and was angry. This was probably the part where, in his frustration, he allowed the orchestra to play with out-of-tune instruments, each player playing independently, and none knowing how to play. This resulted in each player adlibbing in his own tongue and coming to blows with the others. Thus went the effort to understand.

Maybe I should make a prayer of thanksgiving to God whose script dictated that I should yet be alive. Then I thought, "The script is not yet finished and the thanks may be premature. I began to feel selfish for being joyful over something the ten others were denied. The rest of the script might yet contain something the ten would be happy to have avoided.

While sitting in thought, I heard human voices coming from the east, a rapid chatter that was not American. All I had to do was quickly plop into my shelter and watch through a slot between the logs. I released the safety on the pistol and aimed it down the beach. I was amazingly calm.

Two Japs appeared with rifles slung over their shoulders, hands in pockets, jabbering rapidly, and doing a fast march along the water's edge. It was nearly dark and they looked neither right nor left, and appeared to be in a hurry. Had they decided to inspect my shelter, I would have allowed them to come very close before I fired. They disappeared in the west, the sun set, and I began to shake violently. I slumped down in the sand to sleep as the first contingent of mosquitoes filtered in. I left the gun cocked in the slot and covered my face with the coverall as much as it could cover. Whatever was exposed the mosquitoes could have. The worst they could do was to carry off no more than one drop.

Another day dawned. What the hell should I do? Should I proceed westward up the beach or stay put? The prospect of staying in place sounded hopeless and depressing, for it might last for months or even years.

Intelligence officers had indicated that there might be friendly natives on the island. The word "might" was annoying, but we were told that was the best evaluation they could give. The natives on Bouganville were definitely unpredictable, and I was glad not to be there.

Whatever course of action I was about to take, there was one that needed no decision gyrations. It was to eat.

The anticipated menus conjured up no pleasure. I remembered the meal before our last takeoff. It was served at about five o'clock in the morning. We always ate early before a raid because there was so much to do before boarding the planes. The meals were somewhat monotonous, consisting of powdered potatoes, powdered milk, powdered eggs, canned butter, and dehydrated everything that could be dehydrated. Only water was not dehydrated.

The cooks tried to make all servings as appetizing as possible. Sometimes, yielding to various human frailties, they would succumb to too much reinforced fruit juice. Without their realizing it, they would mix powders in the wrong proportions or improperly cook the preparations. The troops would eat their fill grumbling all the way.

On this particular morning the chow was well prepared. I took a usual portion but could not eat. The tension was very great. Everybody was tense before a raid, but pretended calmness. I nibbled a few bits and shoved the plate aside. It had beautifully prepared potatoes, eggs, shredded ham, toast, jam, and butter. Stepping out the door, I had looked back at my plate for I always hated to waste food. This morning facing a feast of raw crabs, coconuts, unknown nuts, and weeds, the vision of that rejected breakfast plate jammed with goodies appeared so real that I reached for it. Then, I blushed with embarrassment.

I headed into the jungle for the nut tree. When I reached it, there was a huge wild boar chomping away at the nuts. We stood and looked at each other for more than a minute. He stood motionless as a rock. I thought about shooting it. There was no way for me to rip it open with my teeth, and I could not cook it. Besides, I'd have to waste a bullet. I decided to leave him alone and gather my portion of nuts.

When I took one step forward, he took one step forward. I took another step forward, he took another step forward and his jaws began to go chomp, chomp, chomp. He had large hooked tusks protruding from each side of his mouth.

I slowly bent down to pick up a nut. He made a loud snort and began to come slowly toward me. I ran as fast as I could which wasn't very fast. When I looked back, he was standing motionless under the nut tree as if he were king of the whole jungle.

I went to the shelter and bashed a coconut, thinking about that breakfast plate I'd left on Guadalcanal. Coconut bashing is a long, tiring effort, and it exhausted me. I sat down in the sand to rest and stare at the ocean and feel sorry for myself.

A thought boomed into my head. Yesterday, it was the noise the Japs made that alerted me to take cover. Otherwise, we might have met eyeball-to-eyeball. Two of them had rifles. I only had a pistol. A very poor match. Back to the shelter I retreated to brood behind the logs.

I began to think about Helen. Gloom and hopefulness lifted a bit. How comforting it was to feel that she was waiting for me. I began to recall and savor words and phrases from her warm and affectionate letters. How sweet life can be. Then came the clanging realization that I might never see her again. I might not leave this island.

This is what war is really like. No chronicle that I had ever read, no story, no movie, no poem had anything to say about what happens to those who fall. When a warrior falls he immediately drops out of sight. He bleeds, but no one ever realizes it. He groans in pain, but is not heard. He may agonize for hours or days, but the story will not come back to him. The playwrights, the poets, the producers will go flying by to present the world with the thrills and romance of the horrible adventure.

Often we had read the reports, "We rejoice over the

great victory we won today. Only one of our aircraft is missing." So the world sings, the victors hoist champagne, and the fallen are forgotten by all but the mothers. And no poet, novelist, composer, or producer pays attention or writes beautiful words about grieving mothers.

I sat in the shelter becoming more and more angry. Finally, I said to myself, "Shit, I'm forgotten, but I'm not dead. Live people do things. I'm going to do something." I decided to abandon the shelter and head westward. I would be brave, but not foolish. I would keep close to the edge of the jungle, keeping ever alert, and ready to jump into the bush at a sign of danger. I became curious about what the Great Script Writer had ahead for me.

Before taking off, I went back to the nut tree hoping the boar was gone. He was. I decided to eat enough for today and for as many days ahead as possible. I made like a camel. Then, with my good friend the stick, I hobbled up the beach.

Whenever a crab came within range, I whacked it and saved the claws. In time I came upon a spot where the jungle reached into the sea. A peculiar tree sent a branch out horizontally. From intervals, shoots grew downward from it to the soil and took root. A new tree developed and grew, but the connection with the original tree remained intact. It looked to me as if this single tree covered an acre and extended into the sea to a depth of between three and four feet. It was impossible to tell where one tree ended and another began because they intermeshed. For anyone trying to pass through, they made a formidable obstacle.

I began to work my way through. It was slow progress because the pain and scabs made the going more difficult. While entangled in this undergrowth, I heard the sweet hum of the motors of a B24. It was wonderful to hear. It flew parallel to the shore at minimum height and minimum throttle. I just knew it was my crew looking for me!

I shouted, but knew it was useless. Desperately I struggled to work my way back to the beach and into the open where I could be seen. I could hear the plane making a turn and returning lower and slower than ever. I could not make it to the open beach. Thinking that it had made its last pass, I quit the struggle and sat down. Then the plane came back a third time. I caught glimpses of it and could see the pilot and two fellows in the waist gun positions.

With the sores and scabs cracked and bleeding, I resumed the effort. At last I was out in the open. I positioned myself at the water's edge, ready to wave my arms and attract their attention. The plane didn't come back. Later, I saw it far at sea climbing for altitude and disappearing.

The Great Script Writer of all human drama did it again. Was I his actor or some kind of a victim from whom he derived a strange pleasure? In spite of this, I felt pretty good because someone bothered to look for me. It must have been my pilot who had recovered from his breakdown and was again flying raids with a replacement navigator. If I had been spotted, a survival parcel would have been dropped and life would have been more pleasant.

I waded into the ocean to wash off the blood and had an idea. Since it was so difficult to pass through the jungle growth, why not go around it since it reached into the sea to a depth of only three to four feet. That's the way I went and reached the other side in about 15 minutes. If I had gone this route in the first place, the fellows in the plane would have seen me. The Great Script Writer is trying to draw the curtains, but I won't let him. I will be my own actor from now on.

After some hours of walking, I came upon a small stream about two feet wide. Before emptying into the sea it created a small pool of clear, clean water some yards into the jungle. I drank the first good water in over a week. It was sweet, or so it seemed. "You never miss water until the well runs dry," I thought to myself.

There was an hour or two of daylight left, and I was drained of strength and emotion. I decided to rest the night on this spot. My stomach said, "What about me?" I had left the nut tree behind and was too tired to bash coconuts. My stomach said, "No excuse."

I had about ten crab claws on the string around my neck. Each had about half an ounce of meat in them. I crushed them with my teeth, sucked out all the nourishment, and spit the bone fragments into the pool. The fragments floated a few seconds before slowly sinking. They attracted some fish that came to the surface to nibble on the particles before they spit them out. Their heads were almost out of the water. Taking careful aim, I shot one. The sound was loud, the splash seemed enormous, but the fish soon floated belly up in the pool.

A vigorous bird chirped and the sound echoed through the wild. Every Jap on the island must have heard it. I seized the fish, hid the spent cartridge, and crawled into the jungle to listen. Except for the protesting birds, all was quiet. No Japs came.

I looked at the fish. There was no alternative. I ate it raw. I debated whether I should go back to the beach after having made so much noise. I was in a situation where there was no other choice. I was compelled to be brave and daring.

"Ah, ha!" I thought to myself. "This is how men win medals of honor. They are put into situations where they cannot reflect, cannot retreat, and are compelled by circumstances to act. The momentum of the action propels him onward. He either survives or vanishes. In either case, he becomes a hero."

It was almost sunset when I reached the seashore and stood gazing at the horizon. I had no thought about how I was to spend the night or fight the mosquitoes. Whatever will be will be, short of being taken by the Japs.

Far out at sea a canoe appeared. As it came closer I was able to count three people in it. In the waning light and because of the distance I could not tell if they were Japanese or island natives. I watched and studied them from behind a tree. Were they Japs or natives? If they were natives, were they friendly or hostile to Americans? After studying them awhile, I noticed a graceful rhythm in their paddling. They moved as if they were born with paddles in their hands and spent a lifetime paddling. They were smooth. Japs would never paddle like that. They were natives!

I hobbled to the water's edge and fired three fast shots. The paddling stopped. For a long time there was no motion. Maybe they couldn't see me in the shadows. I rushed into the water waist deep and splashed. They saw and they came.

I went to the jungle's edge and waited, for they had a long way to come. If they were Japs, I would have crawled into the jungle and hid.

When they were within a hundred yards, I knew they were natives and I came to the water's edge.

Deep in my cranium erupted a nagging concern, would they help me or give me to the Japs? Well, the Great Script Writer already had it in His script, or had he? I envisioned how I'd shoot it out with these fellows if they showed signs of betrayal. This was the tensest moment in my life so far, even more tense than flying through flak and Jap interceptors.

They came to within about 20 yards of me, turned their canoe broadside, and stared at me for some time.

Slowly they began to talk among themselves. Then I perceived that their discussion was turning into an argument.

# Chapter 6

There developed a crescendo in their debate. I concluded things weren't going well. Listening, I could only understand two words they spoke. Over and over again I heard "American" and "Japanese."

"Oh," I thought. "They are arguing as to whether I was an American or Japanese. Why does this make a difference to them? Can't they tell?"

At that time, I was awful in appearance, with a sunburned and peeling face, beard, matted and dirty hair, protruding Adam's apple, and skinny as a string. A grotesque looking creature like me was probably frightening to these people. Maybe they feared me because of the gun. Except their discussion centered on "American" and "Japanese."

Finally, I said, "I am an American. Please come in." When they heard that, they seized their paddles, and drove the canoe onto the beach, jumped out with wide grins, and each hugged me. Next, we shook hands and grinned at each other again and again.

One was short and had shiny black teeth. The others' teeth were normal. They exchanged some fast language and began to throw a hundred pounds or so of potatoes out of their canoe to make room for me. One of them said, "You lay here." Pointing to where the potatoes had been he said, "We gotta go, can't stay."

They paddled with all the speed they could muster,

straight out to sea until we were far out. When they paused to rest, the rim of the sun disappeared below the horizon. One of them said, "We pray now. We pray when sun down."

While the two bowed their heads, one of them chanted a long prayer. This was followed by a hymn that sounded like the hymn in our churches called the "Old Rugged Cross." It was dark when they finished.

I decided to give them my gun thinking that they would feel safer with me unarmed and that it would be a gesture of my confidence in them. They only said, "You keep. You American."

Black Tooth handed me a large pineapple, very ripe and soft like mashed potatoes. The speaker said, "You eat."

With my fingers I scooped out and ate a liberal amount. It was the sweetest and most delicious pineapple ever. It was too big for me to eat it all. I handed back what was left to the Silent One who smiled with pleasure. I will refer to these men as The Speaker, Black Tooth, and Silent One. I could not remember their names from our introductions.

They paddled in beautiful rhythm for an hour or so in the darkness. Suddenly, as if on signal, they turned shoreward. After what seemed like miles and miles of paddling, they hit shore in front of a cave. How they did this in the dark I could not fathom. I asked the Speaker and he pointed to his head and said, "Me think."

The cave extended about five or six paces into a low cliff and was probably six paces wide. There was almost no beach in front of the cave. It was a feat of navigation to hit it in the dark as these natives had done. We had traveled eastward along Choiseul. I had been trudging westward.

As soon as the canoe hit the beach, Black Tooth jumped

out and disappeared to the left, while the Silent One ran off to the right. The Speaker helped me up and guided me into the gloom of the cave to a spot built up with twigs and grasses.

He said, "Lay down. You will like." It was indeed soft and comfortable to lay on. The first decent place I'd had to lie since leaving Guadalcanal over a week ago. I relaxed like I had never before. Never had I realized that mere lying down could be such an overwhelming experience.

After about fifteen minutes, the two who had left returned and began to jabber. They began to laugh freely and often. Laugh! It was great to hear laughter again. There must be something going right that made it possible for these people to laugh. I began to feel good again.

A fire lit up the interior of the cave. It was a beautiful shelter that made excellent protection against storms, rains, and maybe Japs. I could see that it was used often, for it had prepositioned items such as pots, pans, cans, cushioned sleeping mats, and built-up grass areas for sleeping.

I smelled something cooking as jabbering and laughing continued. Each native came to me in turn and asked, "Good?"

"Yes," I said. "Good."

They would laugh heartily and go back to the fire to jabber and laugh some more. It sounded wonderful to hear people laughing. The finest music in the world could not have sounded more beautiful than these people. At the base, people did not laugh unless they drank a lot of beefed up fruit juices.

Before long, they helped me up and sat me down before the fire. By the fire was a long broad leaf covered with boiled meat, open coconuts, roasted potatoes, and piles of cooked greens. They formed a circle around me, chanted a prayer, sang a hymn, and pointing to the coconut said, "Drink!" Next they pointed to the goodies and said, "Eat!" I did, and they sat and watched.

I expected them to eat with me and so motioned, but they only grinned and said, "You eat." The meat was pork, probably wild pig, and tasted great. The greens looked like spinach but were something picked out of the bush. I was hungry. I enjoyed this feast more than the finest banquet.

I motioned when I was finished whereupon they attacked what was left with gusto. I had sensed that they were very hungry but had held off until their guest had finished.

When time came to retire, they arranged their mats in a semi-circle around me and began to sleep. I laid against the wall of the cave and fell asleep. Until I did and any time I awakened, there was a low, slow conversation, punctuated by chuckles and laughs. I felt I was safe and in friendly hands, and a warm and calm feeling settled over my being.

Beams from the rising sun filtered through the bush into the shelter. The three rescuers began the day by chanting a prayer and singing a hymn. After the ritual, one of them trotted into the jungle to the left and another to the right. The third worked on the smoldering embers of yesterday's fire until he coaxed it into sizable flame.

After about fifteen minutes the two men came back with a small bunch of bananas, coconuts, sweet potatoes, greens, and a fish. The fish and potatoes were buried in the hot ashes of the fire. The greens were put in a can and boiled. The bananas were roasted on a stick. Roasted bananas!

When cooked, the food was laid out on a broad green leaf, and I was motioned to eat while they sat in a circle around me and watched. They grinned while I debated how to attack the fish. It was a big one, about 16 inches long. When the ashes were brushed off, there remained a hard shell-like crust formed by the scales. It came off in one piece exposing beautiful white flesh.

I scooped up breakfast with my fingers. They did not talk or move until I had finished. They moved in, ate their fill, and wrapped the leftovers neatly in leaves. They stored them in a fiber bag and placed it in the boat.

The boat was a dugout, carved out of a single, large log. It was large enough to carry four people. I was glad it wasn't a three-man boat.

We began our journey. I sat in the middle on a cushion made of soft grasses. They also made a backrest against which was I was able to lean and ride in a relaxed fashion.

They sat on hard wooden seats, two behind and one ahead. I noticed for the first time that each had a Japanese rifle and a lot of ammunition. They also had a small spear for snagging fish, crabs, and maybe people.

In all their actions, their concern for my every comfort made me feel like a king. I believe I had better treatment and more tenderness and reverence afforded me than the storybook kings, queens, princesses, or emperors who were carried by dozens of servants. It was a surprising phenomenon and a big turnaround in my fortune. All during the past week, just about everything that happened conspired to make life as miserable as possible or even to end it. The coconuts were tough, the crabs were small and quick, water had larvae, mosquitoes were numerous, and the nut tree was guarded by a wild boar.

Because I was an American, these people went all out for my comfort and safety. There was no doubt they were taking a big risk. If the Japanese caught them harboring the enemy, they would make the supreme sacrifice. I sat in the canoe with confused thoughts and watched them perform art with their paddles.

Choiseul is a rather big island and the first island east from Bouganville. The Bouganville we had attacked heavily and the Japs defended fiercely. Personally, I could not understand why they wanted to keep such a place unless it was to make our losses as heavy as possible. I presumed our leaders sent us out to wear them down, and the side that wore down soonest lost. We contested and one of the losers was our crew.

Choiseul was about 80 miles long and roughly 25 miles wide at its widest part. It had a mountain, probably 5,000 feet at its highest, running through the center. I had studied the island thoroughly each time we flew over it with thought about where to go should we be forced down on it. The west end appeared high and dry, while the east end was low, swampy, and apparently uninhabited. The west end and the south coast had most of the Japanese installations on it. I had come ashore on the north coast at about the midpoint of the island and decided to walk westward thinking it would be more eventful than going eastward and getting hopelessly mired in the swamps. I was right, for now as we paddled eastward along the coast, only mangrove swamps lined the shore.

The mangrove trees sent horizontal branches seaward from which shoots grew downward and took root in shallow water. The shoot became a tree and repeated sending out branches that took root, while keeping the connection with the mother tree. The final result was a thick entanglement that was difficult to pass through. The Japanese patrols avoided passage through areas of mangrove growths. The downward shoots were in three to four feet of water, and were spaced so that it was possible to pass through with a canoe. We canoed along the edges of the mangrove growths.

I became absorbed in the rhythm and endurance of these men. They paddled for at least an hour before even a pause. They began in silence. Gradually, a hum of some rhythmic tune developed. After some time of humming, one would burst out into song and the rest joined. This went on until noon, about five hours.

They put the paddles down, said a long prayer, and pushed their way through the mangroves to shore and dinner.

As before, they allowed me to eat first while they sat around and watched. Only when I was through did they touch any food. They ate what I left. The fish, the potatoes, and the roasted bananas were finished.

Again they went out of their way to make me comfortable and fed. They kept asking if I had had enough to eat, if the seat was comfortable, and if I was too tired. If I moved, they would come and ask if there was anything they could do to help. I was certain that the Queen of Sheba with all her servants, slaves, and subjects did not receive such attention. Maybe my awful appearance stimulated a certain amount of sorrow for me. But I finally concluded they were just that kind of people.

After a prayer, a hymn, and a short rest, I was seated like a king, as high in the dugout as possible. We fought the mangroves to the sea. This time there was much excited conversation that gradually tapered off into rhythmic hum, then spirited rhythmic song.

The songs were hymn-like tunes which sounded like, "Swing Low Sweet Chariot," "Onward Christian Soldiers," and the like, sung in time with the paddle strokes.

In perfect rhythm and without pause, they paddled for hours. It seemed they were born with a paddle like a fish is born with fins.

We did not go far out to sea. The Speaker said, "We safe by shore. Much jungle." The jungle extended past the shoreline and into the sea, an area the Japanese avoided. If I had ventured in the eastward direction, I might have never been found for years.

By evening, after about six hours of paddling, we began to round the east end of Choiseul. We were in the passage between Choisuel and Santa Isobel Island. We'd covered, by my navigational instinct, about 40 miles. When the sun touched the horizon, the men placed the paddles down, bowed their heads, and chanted a long prayer followed by a hymn.

Before bringing the canoe ashore, two men jumped into waist deep water. Wading ashore, one crept cautiously up the beach to the right and the other to the left. We had come out of the mangrove swamps onto a sandy shoreline. The Speaker and I waited offshore until the scouts came back. Apparently, all was safe and after about 15 minutes a signal to come in was given.

My rescuers went into action with seemingly rehearsed precision. One went to work building a shelter, one to making a fire without matches, and one to spearing fish, clams, and crabs. Again, we enjoyed roasted yams, bananas, fish, and coconut milk.

These fellows had a marvelous skill at opening tough coconuts. While holding the nut in their hands, they delivered several vigorous, precision chops with a machete across the end making an opening for drinking.

As before, the best fish, potatoes, bananas, and whatever else were offered to me. They ate what was left.

When time came to sleep, they allowed me to sleep in a shelter made up of short poles, broad leaves, several rolls of woven mats, and burlap type blankets that they carried in their boat. From its construction it seemed the shelter was intended to offer comfort by keeping out the abundant mosquitoes. It was warm enough to sleep in the open. When satisfied that I was safely retired, they sat in front of the shelter talking and laughing far into the night.

These were black people, of medium height, with kinky hair, sharp noses, and thin lips. The Speaker was well built, broad shouldered, strong looking, and probably in his mid-twenties.

Silent One was an elderly man with a thin, wiry body. He was an avid talker and a joke teller. I called him Silent One because he knew no English and tended to all my wants in smiley silence.

Black Tooth was taller than the others and smoked a pipe every chance he could.

They seemed to love jewelry. Each wore a necklace made up of snail shells and a variety of colored pebbles and fragments. In their pierced ear lobes they stuck various small blossoms or, lacking these, grasses tied into fancy knots.

For clothes they had very brief jockey-type shorts covered by a burlap-appearing cloth wrapped one-and-a-half times around their waist and secured with twine. They wore no footwear.

Each carried a knife that seemed like the most useful thing they could own. The tobacco smoker carried his ingredients and equipment in a belt around his waist. He had matches but used them for lighting his pipe. He rubbed sticks for making a campfire.

The Speaker knew English. A type of English that was universal throughout all the islands in the South Pacific. It was called Pigeon English. It was a language stripped of everything but the barest essentials.

For example, if we meant to say, "Let us go into the house," by this language we'd say, "We to house go." Or, if we wished to say, "Cook me some potatoes because I am hungry," we'd say, "Cook potato, me hungry." Another example, "Let us not talk so much. When the war is over, then we will talk." would come out, "No talk. Fight finish, talk."

Once accustomed to such communication, ideas could be exchanged effectively. It was easy to learn, and The Speaker and I enjoyed kidding each other. I enjoyed this unique manner of conversing.

I could not keep from wondering why I, an American, was treated so well by these black people living on islands I had never heard of before. I figured they'd never heard of America either.

They were doing this at some considerable risk and seemed ready to engage in a firefight with the Japanese to defend me. It also had cost them a boatload of potatoes.

A feeling of self-consciousness came over me, a humble feeling mixed with guilt when I remembered the fellows who did not make it.

At home I was a backwoods, stump-pulling muzhik to whom very few would give an ear. Here, to strangers, I was a king. I was tempted to say, "Stop. Take it easy. Let me be." Then again, maybe they were not doing all this for me, but for an American and what America was all about. Yes, maybe they were doing this for an American, and not just for Frank. I accepted this notion.

What, in the eyes of these people, was there about Americans that was worth saving my butt at this critical time? These were black people. Some Americans had awful weird notions about the black people in their midst.

I recalled an episode involving a black soldier who was from the north and not yet familiar with southern ways. He boarded a bus and took a front seat. The driver glared at him, said nothing, but simply settled back into his seat.

The passengers soon became impatient and began to make uncomplimentary comments about him. Whereupon, the driver stood up and said, "As soon as this nigger goes to the back of the bus where he belongs, we'll get moving." The passengers, mostly northern GIs, were momentarily surprised and hushed. Southern passengers began making hostile noises against the black soldier, who reluctantly went to the back, and the bus moved.

The back part of the bus was usually filled with exhaust fumes, but not much was done about it. I was angry over the incident, but because I was shy I hadn't the courage to speak. The consequences would have been being called a "nigger lover," which was a very undesirable label. If I'd persisted in standing up for the black person, I'd have placed myself in a position similar to that of a rabbit in a room full of owls.

I wondered what would have happened if a black man had some how landed among these white people and was in mortal danger. How would he have been received? Here I, an American, was received and protected like an English monarch. There must be something good about Americans. Something that these people quickly learned about and responded to by their treatment of me.

Next morning, from the position of the rising sun, I concluded we were on the southeast tip of Choiseul. I estimated the date to be between November 4 and 8. Just before sunrise, Black Tooth and Silent One ran off in opposite directions along the beach to reconnoiter, and returned in time for the sunrise religious service. This morning, breakfast preparations and departure were more hurried than usual.

There were no longer mangroves into which we could quickly dart to hide. The shoreline was mostly a white, wide sandy beach broken only by the occasional reach of the jungle into the ocean.

Before seating me as low as possible in the canoe, the three looked over the peeling sunburned skin in my scalp and the large scabs behind my knees and asked me how I felt. The hole through my calf had ceased to be red and festering. The sulfanilamide medicine was working wonders.

Each expressed a deep sympathy and acted as if they themselves were suffering the pain. I loved these guys. I wanted to throw my arms around them, but was not sure if their customs permitted such a gesture. Several times The Speaker repeated, "We sorry you hurt."

With me almost lying in the boat, they paddled probably two miles straight out to sea before setting course parallel to shore. They settled into their usual easy rhythm, started humming a tune, then sang a song keeping time to the paddle strokes. I was amazed at the tunes. Some sounded like "The Battle Hymn of the Republic" and "Marching Through Georgia". Of special surprise was a tune that was popular in the States at the time. It went like,

*"I love somebody*
*Oh yes I do*
*I love somebody*
*But I won't tell who."*

It had a rhythm that went well with what they were doing.

To the south in the distant haze appeared the islands of Kolombangara and Vella Lavella. They were about 20 miles away. We were in the waters then known as "The Slot" in which some big naval battles and the PT 109 incident had occurred.

War signs were becoming evident on Choiseul, shattered trees, beached and sunken barges, and crashed airplanes. In time, I began to wonder where we were going. Till now I totally surrendered to these three men feeling, what will be will be.

I asked The Speaker, "Where we go?"

He said, "To village. Safe. Rest."

He named the village. Its name has left my memory. It was about 25 miles westward from the eastern tip of Choiseul.

Sometime in late afternoon and about two to three miles at sea we arrived at a point opposite the village. They put down their paddles and strained their eyeballs studying the shore. I could see a number of large straw-like buildings scattered throughout a clearing in the bush. It seemed deserted.

A single-engine airplane had crash landed and lay on the beach. For a long time we sat motionless looking at the shore. I thought they were waiting for nightfall.

Finally, a native appeared out of the bush and came to the water's edge. He and my rescuers exchanged signals that I did not understand. When finished, we made a fast run to shore.

I was formally introduced to the newcomer whose name was Tomsoy. He was a young man, probably in his mid-twenties, well built, muscular, red-haired, and about five-and-a-half feet tall. He took my hand in both of his and shook it, and shook it, while looking at me and acting as if I was his long-lost father.

In the meantime, The Speaker uttered one fast sentence about five minutes long. The Silent One cut in and repeated it. Black Tooth took his turn and the whole affair took on the aspects of a long-sought reunion. Conversation was lively, animated, and full of laughter. From gestures and eye movements, I guessed that the discussion was mostly about me.

Tomsoy began to examine my person as if he were a doctor. He looked at the blistered sunburned scalp and moaned as if it was he himself who hurt.

I was still wearing only my flying coverall. In flight, this garment was worn over clothing selected for the high altitude cold. It now hung over a bare, thin body, and appeared to be a dozen sizes too large.

"This is all I have," I said.

"Oh!" He said laughing and sad at the same time.

"We find you better clothes." Then he noted that I walked stiff legged and asked, "Why you walk funny?"

I showed him the scabs behind my knees. He moaned in pain.

"We make medicine," he said.

The village of about 20 pole buildings, some quite large and artistically covered with a variety of palms leaves woven in intricate patterns, extended about a third of a mile along the seashore. Each building was constructed on stilts with the floor, made of tightly spaced round poles, about four feet above the ground. They were about 20 by 20 feet and larger.

About an hour or so before sundown, my three rescuers hastened away into the bush, each in a different direction. Tomsoy took me to what appeared to be the most elaborate house in the place. It was probably a country club where these people entertained themselves in peacetime. Now, it was pretty bare, stripped of most of what was considered valuable.

Still, a few artistic things hung about, bearing testimony to more pleasant times. There were woodcarvings, designs, and figures woven out of fibers of various sorts. Three feet above the floor and surrounding the complete perimeter of the room was a shelf about three feet wide made of poles and woven mats.

The entire building, as well as the furniture and accessories, was built of poles, woven panels, and woven mats. These were all held together with fibers. The structure was very rigid, but there wasn't a nail or a bolt anywhere. In the structures throughout the whole village there were signs of an artistic urge on the part of the builders.

Tomsoy pointed to an area on the shelf and said, "You sleep here. We make good for you. We make sleep nice." It was a place on the shelf, built to be springy, and covered with several mats made of woven coconut leaf fibers. Not very cozy, I thought, but compared with what I had been sleeping on, it was luxurious.

We went outside, walked to the edge of the beach, and sat down. It was peaceful and quiet and one would not suspect there was a violent war in progress.

Due south in the hazy distance, I could dimly make out the island of Vella Lavella, and to the left of it and more distant was Kolombangara. I recalled how we had attacked those islands. Now, they looked peaceful.

There was no other soul in this village but Tomsoy and I. Normally, I estimated 500 people populated this place. This included families, squealing children, and dogs. It was abandoned. Tomsoy watched me and sensed what I was wondering about. He explained. "In March last year Jap come. He don't like native people. He take from garden. He bother our women and take our house. We fight. He kill. We cannot fight gun. We all run and hide far in bush. Jap cannot find. We watch Jap. We hide. Sometime Jap leave men alone. We go fishing in ocean. Men come to village sometime. When Jap come, we go. We have gun now. Sometime kill Jap. We hide em good."

He pointed up the beach to a spot where the tip of a propeller and rudder protruded from the water and said, "Him Jap plane. Jap inside." He talked on in slow Pigeon English about what war had done to native life, and how he was happy to help Americans get the Japanese out.

People coming out of the jungle interrupted our conversation. They came straight to me and shook my hand, looked me over, and grinned. They seemed pleased to have touched an American.

They kept coming in by fours and fives until there were three dozen of them. They all shook my hand. They also wanted to say something but had no mastery of Pigeon English. So they said something that I took to mean, "I'm glad to have you here." Tomsoy later confirmed that is what they said.

Each one brought something. They came loaded with things to eat and began to lay the ground out for a feast. One brought me clothing, some under shorts, an undershirt, some Australian military trousers, and a shirt. They brought no shoes.

Another group laid out a bed complete with a pillow, sheets, and a blanket.

Also, broad leaves were laid out on the ground like tablecloths. Placed in one area was a gleaming white dish with knife, fork, spoon, and cup. These were the only utensils in sight.

How strange it was to see something from the industrial world intermingling with their simple and primitive one.

Though life and the surroundings of these people revealed a quiet simplicity, they were not unaware of what went on in far away places or what was available there. I was somewhat surprised when one of the natives approached with a tin of pleasant smelling ointment. He handed it to me and said, "This good. Put on sore. Feel nice." I took it and did as he instructed. He watched and seemed very pleased.

The big red sun was about two diameters from the horizon when, after all kinds of activity and good-natured razzing of each other, a meal was ready. Tomsoy said, "We make big eat for you. Everybody say they sorry you have much sore. We want make you strong, cover up all bones."

Indeed, there laid out on large leaves on the ground was a simple, beautiful, south sea gourmet dinner for about 30 people. At each place was a roasted fish, roasted bananas, sweet potatoes, tomatoes, some kind of greens, and coconuts. On my plate was the biggest and best fish of all, as well as the best of everything else.

Tomsoy said, "Sun low. Eat ready. We pray."

Then a strange thing happened. As if on signal, the fellows formed three separate circles. Tomsoy explained that it was prayer time and that one group was Catholic, one was Protestant, and one was Seventh Day Adventist. I was welcome to join any group.

I followed him to the Catholic group and sat down on the ground. One man stepped into the center of each circle and began religious services. They preached, chanted, sang hymns in all manner of loudness, made responses, stood up and sat down. Each acted according to their denominational ritual. Though the groups were close to each other, none seemed to interfere with the others. These were very religious and Christian people.

The services were over in about 20 minutes and all groups rose and intermingled with the others. I couldn't tell who belonged to which group. How peculiar, I thought. How alike these natives looked, how they worked together in harmony, how they lived together, and how they quickly sorted themselves out on the basis of an idea. They all felt a longing to pay homage to their

Creator, but each did it in his own way without arguing about it.

Each man sat down on the ground opposite his measure of food. One man stood up and, looking at me, gave a short speech while all the others looked at me with small smiles. From this I gathered that he was talking about me.

When it was over, he sat down and Tomsoy explained the address saying how pleased all of them were to have me, an American, eating with them. I was to eat first. I did, while they waited. The more I ate, the more pleased they seemed. The fish, which was roasted in hot ashes, was very tasty.

It was a large fish. I was able to consume only a small part even though I ate a great deal. Finally I said, "I am full." They let out a small cheer, seized what was left on my plate, divided it among themselves, and made quick work of the portions. In these people's world, this must have been an ultimate of banquets, as great to them as the feasts of the monarchs of Europe. All this was in honor of me, an American muzhik.

# Chapter 7

Ever since I was picked up by these people, somewhere deep in my consciousness was a nagging feeling these people were giving me the royal treatment so that I would lose all caution. Then, they'd eventually give me to the Japs. I hated the thought, but it lingered. Continuously, I looked for signs that might give away to my eventual disposal. At times, I felt myself on a limb in a world armed with saws.

But on this evening, I dropped all caution and gave myself to the "bosom of Abraham." These people were sincere, and it would be pure shame to suspect them.

Another thought came to mind, "What is so special about being an American?" America must mean something real different from what these natives perceived of the world outside their own. I began to feel good about our country. Somebody outside likes us. These people, of whom I knew nothing before I came here, knew enough about us to like us and give help when in trouble. A warm feeling of love for these people enveloped my being. As of this moment, concentration and effort shifted away from pure survival and powerlessness. I felt hope and that I had a future. It was dark when Tomsoy said, "Time sleep. This way come."

On the shelf assigned to me were white sheets, a blanket, and wonder of wonders, a military mosquito net. I crawled into it while the remaining space filled with natives until there wasn't a square foot left. They unrolled fiber mats and covered themselves with a rough, burlap-looking blanket. Some used wooden pillows. Mosquitoes seemed to avoid them with the same vigor as they were attracted to me.

Some three dozen sleeping men filled the hut to capacity as silence oozed into the atmosphere. Then, sounds of breathing began, all sorts of sounds and pitches, but no real snoring.

It was amusing.

Because there was so much to think about, I could not fall asleep right away. If I thought these men were all fast asleep, I was wrong.

Someone in the darkness thought of something to say. It sounded like, "Kus che ina padarita kud keshane ish draskita." After a few seconds others made acknowledging sounds from different parts of the room, "Uph" "Zee voo" "Grundo" and "Eklop".

After a few minutes, someone else thought of something to say, "Ash nieko nezhino. Tu ir nieko nezhiner Mes visi quveili."

Again, acknowledging, "Kezow" "Oh wool" "Grunt" "Spzvus" and so on from a dozen sources.

This went on all night. It seemed that whenever someone had something to say he said it, then and there. There was no waiting until tomorrow.

Often laughter bubbled out of the crowd. Even though I didn't understand what was said, I laughed when they laughed, because I felt good again. There was going to be a future, another chance. These people were amusing, friendly, and different.

At sunrise, the men sorted themselves out into three denominational groups for religious ceremonies. Each sang hymns loudly and vigorously, but didn't seem to interfere with the rituals of the groups next to them.

Then, they rose and slowly and lazily trudged off into all directions except seaward. About half a dozen remained. They prepared a meal of fruit, potatoes, and greens.

With breakfast over, Tomsoy said, "Today you rest here. Tomorrow, tomorrow, and tomorrow. Then we go to safe place. Two men go fish. Two go hunt. Two stay here. "

Tomsoy and a fellow named Umburu stayed. They sought out a comfortable place under a coconut tree and went to sleep, while I explored the full length of the village. There were signs that this was once a well-populated and busy village, with gardens full of flowers and vegetables. It was now abandoned, with scars of war evident in shattered and bullet riddled trees.

There was some heavy strafing done here by American planes using 50-caliber bullets. There must have been something here for them to shoot at. Then, I remembered I was in enemy territory.

Since I was tired, Tomsoy said I should rest. I went to the seashore and sat down. There was a warm smell of the sea in the air, a soft hiss of waves against the shore, and birds exercising a language in the bushes.

Slow thoughts began to glide through my cranium. How can people be killing each other by the thousands in a world as beautiful as this? Lions or elephants don't do that, and they are dumb. A few days ago I was in the clang, bang, roar of the war. In a flash, I'd fallen out of it like a grain from a brick in a big construction project to be trampled into the ground.

A black cloud of loneliness descended. My thoughts raced halfway around the world to home and my parents. Visions of their grief brought tears to my eyes. I knew Mother's tendency toward pessimism. By now she had to be certain I was gone. When I left home she'd said, "If you go into the Pacific and if anything happens, you will fall into the water and the sharks will eat you up. You won't get away from them. Nobody does."

I had said, "I just might be in a boat."

She said, "No, there are no boats on airplanes."

As she visualized it, any disaster was final.

At this point, I was happy that this wasn't so. As for Dad, he in his peasant toughness, I pictured him moving about mechanically in stony, numb silence. He would be doing things through habit, without feeling purpose for what he was doing.

Thoughts about Helen settled onto me. I longed for her companionship, to be touching her, to be noticed by her, and to be hearing her. In the last two years, I hadn't seen her for more than one week. Our letter writing had begun during my lonesome moments at Camp Livingston, Louisiana. I wrote a cautious and correct letter asking if she would consent to corresponding with me. She promptly answered in a formal way that she would be glad to. This boosted my morale and gave me strength to face whatever might come.

I have always been shy about girls, finding it difficult to relax with them. Experiences with girls during my formative period had been somewhat jarring. When starting kindergarten, I did not know a word of English. Children, most of them girls, laughed loudly because I "talked funny." I learned to be defensive in their presence.

By third grade I had mastered the English language and confidence grew. A new girl enrolled in my class. She was pretty and carried herself in a manner that kindled certain feelings of warmth and affection.

I wanted her to notice me as much as I noticed her, but she remained cool toward me.

As time went on, pressure began to build for me to make an overture toward her. Since she sat in the seat directly to my right, I decided to write her a long note, and I did. It was full of terms of endearment meant only for the eyes of my one and only. It was private stuff.

With reluctance and my feelings tugging at my arms trying to stop me, I did it. I handed her the long note, a violation of the teacher's no-note-passing rule.

As she read the note I was looking for a faint smile or, maybe, a coy glance. I expected a slightly warm note in return. I wanted to be something to her. Tension was building up along with my expectations.

Eventually, without looking at me, this object of my affection went straight to the teacher and handed the note to her. Without looking at me, she returned to her seat.

The teacher pretended fury at the breach of her edict and the impropriety of the contents of the note. She raged, "Frank you will lose recess time, noon time, and you'll remain after school." She then put my name on the blackboard under the list of misbehavers. She wrote it larger than the rest.

As if that weren't enough, she took the note and tacked it on the bulletin board with four tacks. She announced to the rest of the pupils, "I want you to notice what naughty things this boy wrote to a nice girl."

The note hung there all the next day. All the kids eagerly read it. In the manner of children who have not yet learned to restrain themselves, they laughed in a screeching manner. This exposure of my bare and vulnerable soul put me into a brooding mood for a long time. As for me, I could find no way to shrink down to invisible size.

A few days after this, we were assigned to memorize some Mother Goose rhymes and other poems, among which was this little ditty:

> *What are little girls made of?*
> *Sugar and spice and everything nice.*
> *What are little boys made of?*
> *Snails and rails and puppy dog tails.*

I sat and listened to kids reciting it and could make connection between it and what happened.

This episode taught me to be cautious with girls, not to reveal how I felt, and to talk to them very little.

Nevertheless, I often liked what I saw, and secretly nurtured affection and was cautious and proper whenever I said anything to them.

It so happened that during the summer of my fourth or fifth grade, a family with three kids came to fish in our lake. One of the kids was a girl about five or six years old. She was black-haired, round faced, and slightly freckled. She had a slightly high-pitched voice, and her clothes were well worn like mine.

It suddenly dawned on me that these were the features in a girl that I liked. A germ of feeling for her began which never disappeared, but grew in the years that followed.

I saw her almost every summer when her parents came to our farm to visit and to fish. Sometimes she, her brother, and I would go out on a boat ride, which to me was a pleasurable event indeed. I loved to look at her at every opportunity, but felt that to her I was just another older guy. In the years that followed, she grew prettier and I grew older.

In my college years, I dated very little, probably because of this particular little girl who now was back home in high school. I wanted to correspond with her in the worst way, but the fear of not receiving an answer caused me to hesitate.

After graduation from college, I thought, I will see her more often. I hoped she would consent.

I went on with the business of calculus, physics, and economics, while Hitler went on with the business of Czechoslovakia, Poland and England.

One day, the President congratulated me on being selected and honored to serve in the Army, an offer I couldn't refuse. I left home in early spring of 1941, and was assigned to M Company of the 128 Infantry Regiment of the 32nd Division. In my heart, where she had been since she was five, came a girl with black hair, round face, small freckles, and a great shape.

★ ★ ★

I wondered what the fellows at Guadalcanal were doing and whether our pilot had recovered in New Zealand. Strange that a fellow so skilled in piloting, so calm in action, and so able in soothing concerns of his crew-members should break down. Perhaps he absorbed the tensions and worries of all of us.

I also wondered about our short copilot, a jolly guy who joked about his concern about dying a virgin.

I thought about our ball gunner, the one with the nastiest job in the whole war. He was suspended below the belly of the aircraft, lying in a curled position for the duration of engagement. He depended on his crewmates to hoist the ball into the ship so he could exit. He could freeze to death if the current to his electric suit was shut off. Yet, knowing all this, he still accepted the job.

There should be a special monument to all ball gunners of this war. Anybody speaking to one should do so in hushed and reverent tones.

I wondered about my things at the base, if they had been packed away and sent home. This was standard procedure for missing personnel. Often I'd assisted in it. Probably the worst thing would be the returning of all letters to senders, especially those from Helen.

After about an hour of reverie, the quiet of the island was interrupted by a sound coming from the east. It sounded like hundreds of motors. So many motors humming was a sound such as I hadn't heard before. Then, they came into view. There were three squadrons of B24s with fighter escort. They were four miles high and flying parallel to the south shore of Choiseul.

Why were they flying over the islands like this when standard procedure was to fly over water to avoid early warning? Tight formation at maximum height meant they were close to bomb drop. I hoped they hadn't picked this village for there was no place to hide. If there were no explosions by the time they were dead overhead I would be safe. There weren't.

I witnessed with a Jap's eye view the possible terror of an American raid. From an American perspective I had viewed it as something beautiful.

It was definitely three squadrons of the 307th Bomb Group. I felt that I could tell by the way they formed up. Besides, in November it was the 307th's turn to operate in the forward areas while the 5th Group operated from Espiritu Santo. These two groups of heavies alternated by flying reconnaissance and supply missions from Santo and strike raids from the "Canal." I even spotted the position of my crew's bomber and concluded that my pilot was back in operation. I'd known it wouldn't take him long to recover. He was just too tough a man.

*The majestic formation moved on*
*With the hum and roar of their great engines*
*Over the steamy land and misty sea below*
*Into hostile black peppered sky before them*
*And the hungry Zeros fought them*
*Through fiery heavens they dashed shiny*
*Until the longed for clean skies opened before them*
*And a homeward course lifted the spirits of blooded souls*
*And Guadalcanal greeted their sons home again.*

★ ★ ★

In a short time, they were out of sight, but the hum of their engines lingered on. "Isn't this like life?" I thought. Silence, then a few moments of sound and fury, then silence again. I was alone and feeling satisfied that I wasn't up there in the cold mean environment being miserable.

There was now time to sit and wonder, and this brought disturbing thoughts. The thought that I hadn't accomplished anything drove me to my first bailout. Here and now I found myself helpless and useless again, unable to do a damn thing.

Up there, some other guy was taking my place and absorbing the dangers that were allotted to me. He may have to take the hurts that were really mine. A kind of guilt saturated my being. Though I feared and dreaded the ordeal of facing flak and Zeros, I didn't feel right having someone else doing it for me. I was not hoping for a role as hero, but the satisfaction of doing my part and maybe at last accomplishing something, even as a horse holder or spear carrier. Now I was a louse in the beard of McBeth.

Two natives appeared from the bush bearing fruit. I gathered that it was noon. They shook my hand and introduced themselves, giving names I couldn't remember. They were not masters of English or even Pigeon English. They looked at me, seeming embarrassed for not being able to communicate like they wanted. They said a short prayer and handed me a meal of fruit. The two proceeded to the foot of a tree and went to sleep.

For the rest of the afternoon, natives kept appearing by twos and threes. They shook my hand, looked me over, made sympathetic remarks, appeared sad, slowly backed off, and proceeded to find a place to sleep.

About 30 or 40 natives came out of the jungle during the rest of the day, until someone was sleeping under every tree in the village. I wondered why these guys weren't concerned about the Japs.

Finally, there came a small, wiry old man who was quite fluent in English. From him I learned much about these people and what was happening on this island as far as the war was concerned.

After introducing himself as "Yousa" and offering sympathy he said, "Come with me because I will show you something." We went to a small clearing just outside the village. There he showed me six graves about a week old. Pointing to each he said, "Here Jap. We kill 'em."

He then proceeded to describe in bloody detail how they did it. I would rather not have heard. Their technique was first to make certain they had sufficient numbers to overwhelm the Japs. They also made sure a good element of surprise was on their side. They wanted to dispatch the Japs in a hurry and without a trace. If these conditions were met, they proceeded. Otherwise, they backed off and let them pass in peace.

I asked if these graves were hidden enough so that the Japanese wouldn't find them and raise hell with the natives. Then came the most surprising bit of news yet.

He said, "Last week an American Army invaded this island at a place called Sangigai. All the Japanese are busy fighting them. They will not snoop around any more. The Americans will take this island away and give it back to the natives."

Joy surged through my body. I tingled at the news. The question about how I was to leave this place was at last answered. The Army would soon come parading down this beach, flag a flyin', band playing, and bayonets shining. Exactly the way they are pictured in the grade school textbooks. I smiled at myself for thinking that way, because I knew things didn't happen that way. Anyway, I visualized a quick ride back to the Canal.

As evening fell the sleepers all awakened from under whatever tree they were sleeping. In small groups all over the village they were vigorously gesturing, talking, and laughing. The volume increased. I wondered how they could find so much to talk about when they did so little.

The talking went on and on while a small busy group prepared a meal in the same manner as the night before. A small speech was made before we attacked the food that Yousa translated as, "We are thankful for the guest we have with us. He is very thin and poor looking but he was once a strong, good-looking, young man. He has hurts all over him. Let us not touch the food until he has eaten his fill. Let's make him enjoy the food. Amen." Probably, the same type of speech they had made the night before. It sounded like it, anyway.

In what was left of daylight, Yousa suggested we go to the seashore to rest and do some peaceful thinking. This Yousa, a small, wiry, stronghold man said, "I like to think. I think a lot. I sit and think after supper." I felt an urge to ask him what he thought about, but didn't. He came to think not to talk. So he thought and I thought, too.

In front of us facing due south was Vella Lavella. A bit farther and in the mist to the left loomed Kolombongara. We bombed the hell out of those islands a few times. To the west of Vella Lavella and into the seas just over the horizon, I had watched a number of B24s go down. Our crew had made thorough searches of that area, but never found anyone. In those waters lie many voices that are still.

*And the stately ships go on*
*To their haven under the hill*
*But Oh for the touch of a vanquished hand*
*And the sound of a voice that is still*

Thus, Tennyson expressed it. Thus, I felt it. I felt a great inadequacy not being able to express in words the thoughts that arose in me. Maybe Yousa did, too.

Finally, as darkness enveloped the land and the sea, we again repeated a ritual that all good people perform in these circumstances. This was the ritual of going to bed.

Once again, the usual chatter continued all night. These people seemed to express their thoughts as soon as they hatched. I slept under a mosquito net. The natives slept in the open.

For four days more, the natives had me rest at this village. Each day Tomsoy and Yousa questioned me and examined my condition. The scabs were darker and drier and were beginning to detach around the edges. "A good sign," Tomsoy would say. We will be leaving as soon as you are better."

"Where will we go?" I asked.

"To a safe place," he said.

"Is this not safe?" I asked.

"No," replied Yousa. "This is a dangerous place. We

have guards on each side of this village watching day and night. If Japs come, we all go into bush."

Since Americans had invaded this island, I was expecting them to appear any day, probably preceded by Japs in retreat. I was thinking about positioning myself in a way so I could watch them run. In the meantime, I proceeded to do what Tomsoy urged me to do. Rest and soak up strength. I still walked stiff
legged, which was a handicap.

The natives who had no immediate or pressing chores slept all over the village, while I sat on the seashore and stared at the far horizon. I liked to watch the sea, even when nothing was happening. The waves had a soothing sound. A number of naval battles had occurred within sight of where I was sitting. When the Japs evacuated Kolombangara and Vella Lavella they unloaded on the beach where I was sitting. Some of their shot-up barges still littered the shoreline. I felt I was on quite a historic spot.

Invisible, except in the mind's eye, was the sea floor littered with broken ships, smashed airplanes, and the bones of vanished warriors. Among the litter was the Big Moose.

There wasn't much to do but think. Tomsoy said, "You rest good." So I rested.

Yousa said, "Think." So I thought.

I noticed that he thought, too. Instead of sleeping like most of the people, he starred at the ocean, sky, and things around him with a contemplative countenance. I figured that if he recorded his thinking, he might rank as one of the world's foremost philosophers.

At any time, I expected Japs to come running helter-skelter down the beach with Americans in pursuit. I expected the native sentries to come dashing into the village with the news.

Instead, the usual trickle of people came, as every day, to shake my hand and express sympathy.

Except for the native people, no one else in the world knew of me, no one in the 307th Bomb Group, 372nd Squadron on Guadalcanal. Like all those resting on the ocean floor, I had vanished. Well, not quite. I had teetered on the razor's edge of eternity, but had not gone over. On the great tally sheet at the base there was probably a notation, "One of our aircraft is missing. Crew presumed dead."

The Great War would go on and the missing parts would quickly fill in like a hole in water. I reflected on every movie I had seen and the stories I had read. Battles raged on and on, and in the end, victory. No poet or no chronicler recorded the eye view of the world as seen by the fallen and dying. There were no odes to the vanquished, no songs. Here I was who had sat on the razor's edge of eternity not doing any more than all the poets heretofore. I sat by the sea, helpless, and thinking of the words of Alfred Lord Tennyson:

*Break, break, break*
*On thy cold gray stones sea*
*And would that my tongue could utter*
*The thoughts that arise in me*

This great poet had problems, too.

*My failing feet have ceased to carry me*
*Here I lay me down to rest*
*A rest that will have no ending*
*Short days ago I cuddled in mother's arms*
*Shouted and laughed - made father proud*

*I loved life and dreamed dreams of far off times*
*And thrilled at young girls warm embrace*
*Made visions of a new world to come*
*But war bugles sounded in the land*
*In clanging of battle a swift sword found me*
*As great armies went charging on*
*Oh God - unfulfilled will be my dreams*
*Useless will be tears on my behalf*
*Nothing will my sacrifice bring forth*
*What value is my death to me*
*Oh life — sweet life — why did God make*
*Heaven so sweet and death so terrifying.*

By evening, the natives began to wake up while others gathered in from the bushes. There was some excitement. I could gather from the higher pitch in their voices. I learned from Tomsoy's translation that the Americans who had invaded this island at Sangigai had withdrawn.

They were gone. Damn! Why did they do that? Did the Japs succeed in pushing them into the sea? There was disappointment in the voices of the people as they went about preparing supper. There was some laughter, but subdued. Their usual routine of prayer and song and retirement for the night was observed at precise times. For me, a cloud of mild despair seeped into my being.

On the fifth day in the village, after what Tomsoy thought was sufficient rest and rehabilitation, we left. Too much risk the natives said.

Suddenly, there were three long canoes on the beach, each with tall projections on bow and stern, and four paddle men. The projections were adorned with ornaments and the skulls of various animals, such as wild pigs, alligators, and large birds. It reminded me of the Norse ships I remembered seeing in history books.

About 50 natives assembled on this crisp, cool morning. With the sun poking through the horizon, they would shake my hand, say something, and patiently wait to see me off. It was very touching for me that so many should go through so much fuss at my departure. There must have been something very right being done somewhere to create such a feeling toward me, an American stranger.

The first canoe with four paddlers took a quarter-mile lead, followed by the second canoe with me in it, and the third about a quarter mile behind. I sat low in the middle with palm leaves on each side to obscure the view from shore.

The men paddled in silence for a time, with precision strokes and rhythm, and without interruption. First somebody began to hum a tune, then the words of a song, and before long, all four men were singing a marching tune in their husky voices. I recognized American tunes, civil war marches, Negro spirituals, and even some British music. It was beautiful to hear.

This continued with seldom a pause until noon. The paddlers, as if on signal, put down their paddles and said a prayer. Then, straight into shore paddled the first canoe followed by the third one.

When ashore they signaled for us to land. This was a rest and rehabilitation break. We did what was natural, ate lunch, and lay around for an hour. The men were tired, for they must have paddled continuously for hours. We were heading eastward along the shore of Choisuel.

I asked where we were going, hoping to hear the word Guadalcanal. One of them said, "To safe place." All I could do was wonder. I was happy we weren't going westward.

We took to sea again. In similar manner we rounded, by sundown, the eastern end of Choiseul. We encountered shallow water and extensive mangroves that the crews seemed relieved to enter. The canoes bunched up and the men began a playful banter among themselves.

The water was full of creatures, and the men often jumped out and captured crabs, clams, and oysters. Some clams yielded up to five pounds of meat. Boiled, roasted, and fried, these would be our supper for the evening.

# Chapter 8

The natives carried a frying pan and a few other cooking utensils. While they ate with fingers and sticks, I ate from a plate with knife, fork, and spoon. These guys thought of everything when it came to my convenience and comfort. I would gladly have eaten with my fingers and slept on the ground. Instead, like in old Europe, the royalty enjoyed comfort and the peasants roughed it. I felt they shouldn't be doing this, that in my country I ranked lower than they. I was a muzhik.

I was surprised when we bedded down in the same cave that we had stayed in when I was first rescued.

I had done nothing but ride all day and was tired. The men had paddled all day, and still seemed energetic. If required, I believed they could paddle all the way to Guadalcanal. I had a mild urge to ask them to do so, but after having done so much for me already, I felt it would have been asking too much.

From sunrise to about a couple of hours before sunset, the next day was much the same as the one before. We canoed westward along the north shore of the island until we came to what the natives called Kumboro Point. There was a rather sizable river near it. We paddled into the river about a mile, frightening numerous alligators and facing down some defiant ones.

The jungle along the stream was at its best, with its roots in the swamp and the treetops arching over the river.

It gave the sensation of being in a tunnel. The birds were unusually vigorous and screamed in a hundred different pitches. It was wild country indeed.

Eventually, we stopped at a place that seemed to me indistinguishable from any other place. I wondered why they picked it. They hid their boats in the waters of the swamp and said, "We walk now."

In single file, with six men in front of me and six behind, we plunged into the bush. We sloshed through swamp for some distance. There was no path, no trail, and no trace of any kind to indicate that anyone had gone this way before. Yet, they trotted on as if they were following a well-marked road.

Soon, the terrain began to slope uphill with space between trees so the men didn't have to force their way through. Shortly, we assumed a march step and began to follow a winding path up a steeper and steeper slope. The birds protested throughout the jungle as the men began to sing marching songs and rhythmic hymns. These people sang anything that involved repeated rhythms.

Up the ascending winding way we went for nearly two hours. I noticed that as the men marched they stepped so as not to leave a path that could be followed. They never stepped in a way that would leave a footprint.

Finally, as darkness began to envelope the country, we arrived at a pinnacle of a small mountain where I saw a large warehouse-looking building on stilts. It was more heavily built than those I'd seem in the village, and some boards had nails in them. There was some outside influence here. Also, I wondered how my escort found this distant place without a path leading to it.

"How did you find this place?" I asked one who spoke a little Pigeon English. He pointed to his head and said, "Me think." That is how they did things, by thinking.

I was not prepared for what I found at this place. Before operating out of Guadalcanal, we were thoroughly briefed about all the islands in the Solomon group. We were required to draw a scale map from memory. We were also told that there were "coast watchers" on these islands and that they could be helpful in emergencies. We were not appraised about who they were, how they were prepared to help, or what resources they possessed.

Our briefing about the natives had been rather vague and not at all reassuring about those on Bougainville. As to the natives of Choiseul, we were told that odds were good that they were friendly. I didn't like the term "odds" and so determined not to bail out over Choiseul. I didn't, but had to swim to it anyway.

Upon our arrival, half-a-dozen men came pouring out of the building to meet us. They began vigorously shaking my hand and going through all sorts of gyrations indicating they were glad to see my escorts.

One of the fellows, a handsome well-built young man, who introduced himself as Gordon, began to converse with me in English much better than my own. He spoke like a cultured Englishman, with deliberate precision. After living for days with people who spoke little or no English, it was like plunging into ice water while hot and sweaty. At first, I thought he was one of our own GIs assigned here. However, that was not the case. He was a true native and the accent was actually British.

He inspected me and seemed sorry about what he saw. He saw disheveled hair peppered with loose, sunburned skin, a two-week growth of beard, sunken cheeks, a long skinny neck with a sharply protruding Adam's apple, a hairy chest with every rib sticking out, bony hands, and bare feet.

"My dear, dear fellow. I would say that you are in need

of a cleanup, a change of garments, and a good hot meal. I'll get these chaps to attend to you," he said.

In quick order, I was bathed in a round wash tub with fresh water and good smelling soap. Then, I was fed a real American meal of canned meat, mashed potatoes, gravy, bread with butter, vegetables, and coffee with cream and sugar. It was a surprise indeed.

Gordon watched without saying a word. He knew that I was relishing the experience of tasting something other than fish, coconuts, crabs, and sweet potatoes. By the time the meal was completely dispatched, about a dozen natives assembled and formed a circle around the table. Apparently, one of their satisfactions was seeing someone accept and enjoy their hospitality. They beamed and chuckled when I made motions and sounds about how tasty things were. These people were beautiful.

It was completely dark when I finished eating and the rest of the men took their places at the table and had their supper. They attacked their refreshments with much gusto and chatter.

Gordon advised them to retire and said to me, "I am sure you had a long journey today and want to sleep." Before I replied, he'd led me to a bedroom dimly lit by a small kerosene lamp. There were three American military cots, opened up and complete with mattresses, sheets, pillows, and mosquito nets. There were also several folded cots stacked in a corner along with mattresses and blankets enough for ten sleepers.

It was an amazing surprise to see these things in this setting after the ultra-simple living the past two weeks. I was not prepared for this. For the first time since rolling out of bed on the "Canal" on the 25th of October, I was lying on a customary American cot with all the luxuries that went with it.

Gordon said it was the 8th of November 1943. He took the lamp and left, darkness swooped in.

I felt very good, warm, cozy, and comfortable as I stared into the darkness. All was silent except for faint sounds of conversation outside and the squawking of night birds.

Shortly, my good feeling went plunging and the grip of guilt took hold like an eagle's talons on a rabbit. What right had I to be so comfortable here when all of my buddies and my crew were still out there risking their butts and getting their asses shot off? There's a guy out there doing what I should be doing. Maybe, he already had his butt shot off. Here I am, trying to feel good about it. Then, there were those ten guys that went down into the watery grave and the grief that it sent home. I became miserable and fell asleep.

In the morning, Gordon and several helpers were bustling around on the porch preparing some chow. A long wooden table surrounded by a variety of blocks and boxes for seats was laid out to feed about a dozen men. They were milling about and laughing and waiting for me to eat first.

They took their places and prayers were said, simultaneously in three denominations. There were about four members per faith, and their chants intermingled so that I wondered if the words were understood by anyone. As usual, everyone waited for me to finish before they began to eat.

I was surprised that such a place as this existed on an enemy occupied island. We'd been briefed about "coast watchers" only to the extent that they existed and produced intelligence. We were also told that they might give assistance to downed flyers if they could find them. Nothing was said of their means, their facilities, or how they could help. They had turned out to be a well-organized, well-equipped group here on Choiseul. Good fortune beamed upon me.

The location was on top of a small mountain, near the center of the island, surrounded by very thick jungle growth. It covered a flat acre with the ground sloping downward rather steeply on all sides.

Two rather large, well-camouflaged buildings on stilts occupied the location. One was a warehouse type, built somewhat in American style. The other was a more open, recreation type building in the native style made with poles, rope, and palm leaves. The warehouse had a large porch where people ate, a storeroom, and a bedroom designed for rescued troops. Wonder of wonders, it had a well-equipped communications room. It was complete with transmitters, receivers, batteries, battery charging generators, fuel tanks, and antenna.

At first, my eyes bulged at the sight of the sophisticated equipment. There were also numerous miscellaneous items, such as a clock with Zulu time, a desk, technical manuals, calendar, writing paper, and a small safe containing code books and other small items. All this gave me a sensation similar to discovering an electric typewriter in Columbus' flagship.

The storeroom was equally surprising. There were foods, medicines, clothes, first aid items, and other things that modern American troops needed. Foods consisted mostly of dehydrated potatoes, eggs, beets, and other eats that could be dehydrated. In sealed gallon containers were butter, bacon, cookies, bread, and the GI's delight, Spam!

A large number of rifles, mostly Japanese, boxes of ammunition, and grenades were piled up at one end of the room. I went outside to shake off the effects of surprise and to absorb a measure of pride, confidence, and security.

All this hadn't been accomplished on short notice, but had required vision, planning, and sweat. I decided we must have some very smart people running this war after all.

About a dozen men were present at all times, some coming and some going, but the number was constant. They mostly slept, played cards, or sang songs. In the evening, they came together and talked, but mostly laughed.

One of the large leafy trees had a platform about 20 feet above ground. Its leaves and branches were trimmed to give a clear view of the ocean about four miles away. Two natives with binoculars watched the sea all day long. Except for the loud scolding birds, the atmosphere was hushed and very peaceful.

Gordon seemed to be in charge, and unlike most of the fellows, he kept busy puttering around with all sorts of things. He assigned a youngster, about 13 years old, to me as an attendant or valet. His name was Palsumboie. He was a bright eyed youngster, had a perpetual smile, and was ever watchful for my needs. Wherever I went he positioned himself so that he would have me continuously in sight. If he anticipated what I wanted, he'd come running to fulfill it. In critical moments, I was never without toilet paper.

Since his command of Pigeon English was good, we communicated well and I was impressed by his simple native child's eye view of life and of the world. One of his greatest pleasures seemed to be teaching me to speak his language when I showed interest. I did show interest, both to please him and to really learn the language. I wanted to understand what they were laughing about.

Other fellows also were eager to teach me, and at times they would point out things and give its name at such a rapid rate that I couldn't remember fast enough. When I mispronounced a word, there would be a prolonged laugh followed by repetition and correction. It was indeed fun, but I believed they enjoyed it more. They were unique people.

At their suggestion, I carried my shoulder pistol at all times, day and night. After soaking in salt water, it rusted horribly even after each day's cleaning. The ammunition needed polishing constantly.

Even with plenty of time available, I tired of cleaning it every day. I decided to disassemble it and boil it in soapy water. Palsumboie quickly procured a pot, sudsy water, and a fire. While the weapon was boiling, I stirred it as if I were making soup. Palsumboie looked puzzled and didn't understand why I was doing this. He asked. "For fun," I said. "I'm making pistol soup."

Unsmiling he remarked, "Oh! Pistol soup," as if he really believed it.

Soon others came to look and ask. To each I joked, "I'm making pistol soup." Each made the same exclamation, "Oh, pistol soup," in such a manner as if they seriously believed it. I began to feel guilty for fooling them like this. Each would leave with such a serious countenance.

I was finishing the boil when I noticed that the natives had assembled near the recreation building and were laughing. I asked Gordon what was so funny. He said, "You told them you were making pistol soup and you thought they believed it." What a thing to laugh at! Anyway the joke was mostly on me. Gordon informed me that they do not like to laugh in the face of people they like, but laugh afterwards. I reassembled the gun, polished the ammo, washed the holster, and prepared to see if it had done any good. In the days that followed there was no rusting.

There were the usual prayers at noon and supper along

with the meals from the GI stores. At about 8:30 local time, Gordon said that it was time to send the daily radio report and asked that I sit in with him.

At a certain hour and minute each outpost on almost every island in the Solomon's called in a routine report. In urgent situations the message would go out as soon as possible. Gordon composed his message for the day including notification of my arrival, my name, serial number, and a request for instructions. He then encoded it and sent it out by voice, letter by letter. The message looked something like this:

AMCRQ FJZMU WRSHO ECPSG NOFSD BLQSI HJKPT UAVTW TZOAC STRER SPAOZ and so on.

The naval station on Tulagi received, decoded, and sent back a coded response. Gordon would decode and execute. In this case a question was sent. What was my condition? Gordon responded Very underweight, with good appetite. Sores healing satisfactorily. Answer. Keep him there until further notice. End of message.

At last, the world outside knew I was alive. It was the 9th of November 1943, or 15 days after the crash. "From here on," I thought, "things will begin to move swiftly." I almost felt the wheels of a vast machine beginning to turn faster and faster eventually culminating in my rescue. I was sure it would be no more than two days hence.

Pulsumboie had the bed ready, and I jumped in with good spirits. I started thinking. The longer I thought the more upset I became. "Damn them," I thought. "They didn't come to rescue me the morning following the crash." That was usual procedure. I was spotted and surely a report had been radioed. Surely, that was done.

No one showed. Maybe they thought that no one could survive a night in shark-infested water. Why waste the effort?

At the base on Ka1i Field, the thinking probably had gone something like this. "The Navy received the message. They have the seaplanes. They'll take care of it. We'll wait for them to pick up the guy. We do not have the means to trundle over to Choiseul to pick up this guy however we may want to. Tomorrow we have this raid to do. We would need a boat or a seaplane. It's the Navy's job."

The message suggested that I wait. With improved spirits and on top of this little piece of world, I settled to do so. I had good provisions and wonderful, good-natured people to be with.

Every day, new people came to shake my hand and offer best wishes. Most seemed shy about not being able to talk with me in my language. I was equally frustrated, for I wanted to make them feel good for their kind thoughts.

I soon discovered that one of their greatest pleasures was my expression of gratitude when I accepted the things, or good wishes, that they offered. They accepted, with a big show of pleasure, things given to them. They'd talk about it excitedly for quite some time afterward.

They loved jewelry of all kinds, and the men adorned themselves with all kinds of it. The women wore very little or none.

The war had caused them to cut down on much of their body decorations. Often, however, they put weeds or flowers in their pierced ear lobes and hair, and hung strings of beads made from colorful seashells around their necks.

For clothing, they wore burlap-like cloth wrapped twice around their waists and that was all. They said that this was their austerity dress because of upsets due to the war. In peacetime they used colorful printed calicoes purchased from Chinese traders that toured the islands.

After jewelry, they highly valued hunting knives, tobacco pipes and tobacco, hatchets, fishhooks, trinkets of all sorts, house decorations, and colored cloth. The war introduced them to more modern items such as flashlights, radios, machetes, and pistols.

Perhaps, what won the hearts of these people for Americans was their experiences with airmen they helped rescue. The airmen gave them some of the special things they possessed. This included highly valued knives, hatchets, fish lines, hooks, and trinkets carried by aircrews as gifts to potential rescuers.

Americans also never touched or took anything belonging to these people without asking or paying. Quite the opposite of Japanese conduct. What would have happened if the Japanese had been kinder? Maybe, if they were kinder, they might never have invaded these lands. They came without being invited and took over.

Religion played a big part in the lives and conduct of these people. I did not see a single person that did not vigorously participate in prayer sessions. Never did they attempt to urge me to attend the services, they welcomed me when I did join.

Denominations were the same as those in Christian countries. Services were conducted in their native language. The hymns were the same as those in our churches. I recognized "Old Rugged Cross," "Swing Low Sweet Chariot," "Rocking My Soul in Bosom of Abraham," "Onward Christian Soldiers," and other songs whose titles I didn't know, but recognized. These people seemed to live and conduct themselves very closely to the dictates of the religions whose ceremonies they practiced. Their faith was strong. Life was simple. The golden rule was their guide.

I watched from the first day we met, how faithfully they conducted rituals to pay homage to their Creator. I was impressed at their gift of faith and their ability to feel the need and presence of God in their lives. I had, in my youth, been quite religious. As years passed I found myself questioning things that religion could not satisfactorily answer.

From time to time, I went to church, attended catechism classes, discussed various questions, and accepted explanations. To many questions the answer was, "You must accept this on faith." This was difficult, and somehow did not penetrate to the center of my soul. Apparently, God had not given me that certain something whereby I could see Him and fully understand His ways. He gave me a mind to ask a lot of questions but not accept the answers that were available. Often, there were no answers available. I constantly struggled for a faith. As I watched these simple native people pray from the depth of their souls, I felt short-changed.

During my third year in college, I had a stroke of good fortune. Our rooming house landlady assigned me a roommate named Joe. He was a stocky, medium-height, young fellow, quite good looking, and with a truly high-output, eight-cylinder mind. By comparison, I was a four-cylinder performer and not all cylinders worked all the time.

Very soon, he took a liking to me for whatever attributes he perceived. We talked, argued and debated issues as though I was his equal. He took my views seriously and pondered them. He never explained exactly what it was, but he claimed that meeting me had changed his ways and outlook on life.

As for me, I felt more influenced in my outlook toward scholarly attainment. I looked upon literature as an obstacle to be hurdled on my way to a degree. Joe pointed out that literature was an artist's explanation of life. I began to like it and took special interest in poetry.

We discussed mathematics and its place in the scheme of the universe. I pursued math with greater interest when he explained that mathematics is the Creator describing how the universe is working.

This led to a discussion about the nature of the Creator, his existence, and his wisdom. We raised questions, answered some, and left some most crucial ones unanswered. One was, "Does a human have a soul?" Some clergy were definitely positive about it, but the Big Book sheds no light on it. We went on to the wisdom of creating man with the characteristics that he has. If the Creator was wise, then why did so many people suffer? Why wasn't suffering evenly distributed?

Often bodies are diseased and in pain, but the mind is clear and sharp causing more suffering. Great men who had much to offer humanity were often killed or treated brutally. Lincoln, who had a plan for a more noble country, was shot. Bruno, who claimed the earth rotated, was treated brutally. Galileo, who contradicted the church, was persecuted. Copernicus, who discovered that the earth was a speck in the universe, did not dare to publish his findings. It only became known after his death.

Could an intelligent Creator make a world whose law for living things is a ruthless and restless struggle for existence? A world in which the powerful, cunning, and unscrupulous and not the nice and genteel survive? Would a God in a universe so infinite be overly concerned about as insignificant a speck as earth? Why doesn't the clergy come to terms with Darwin or the half-life of uranium that measures the lifetime of the planet? Why was Beethoven, who needed ears, allowed to become deaf, or Dr. Johnson, a great speaker, made to lose his voice?

We should be thankful for the good fortune that befalls us. Often during the services, I felt the need to thank the Lord for delivering me from the deep waters, even though He didn't make it easy. The thought kept booming through my head that there were ten men who had not been so favored. Any thankfulness on my part would be selfishness indeed.

I had the feelings I had when I was at sea. I'd felt I should have called, "Lord save me, save me." At the same time I dreaded his rebuke, "You ungrateful fellow. Think of those other crewmembers. You want me to treat you special. Some of those other guys were finer stuff than you. You ask for more than they received."

I couldn't ask for favors or be thankful for good fortune while struggling in the water. Nor could I ask during the services on this safe on solid ground. At the moment, I felt thankful and grateful for things I was enjoying. I was careful that someone else at the same moment was not denied the same goodies. For bad fortune, I could but refrain from a resounding "son-of-a-bitch."

After receiving official acknowledgment of my existence, I settled down to wait for a quick rescue. The date was November 10 or 11, 1943. Gordon and Pulsumboie hustled about tending to my comforts. Others went about taking turns doing alert activities and sleeping. Even at this slow pace of living, there always remained an atmosphere of tension and watchfulness.

Men kept going out and others returning at scheduled intervals. This indicated organized patrols. Those that returned went to sleep, and those who slept, awakened and went out.

The returnees came to Tomsoy, who seemed to be in charge of this activity, to jabber out their stories. Gordon explained that a story was filtering through the island that the Japanese were crowing about how they hurled the Americans back into the sea with big losses at Sangigai. This seemed puzzling to the natives who appeared somewhat disappointed. Hearing reports such as this made it a bit uneasy for me to talk with them.

However, in a few days, word came over the radio transceiver of big American victories on Bougainville. The news brightened the eyes of the people. It also helped me straighten my back and lift my head.

The thought of my prompt return to the 372nd Squadron, 307th Bomb Group of the 13 Air Force had a buoyant effect. More frequently, bigger bomber formations flew overhead, indicating that we were vigorously pursuing the war. There were more bombers in the big blue yonder, not fewer.

Everyday, new people appeared to look at me and shake my hand. Most were able to say a few words in English and expressed sympathy for the crew and my condition. I still looked rough and rugged. A good shave would have done much for my looks. There were plenty of razors but no blades. These guys loved the sharpness of American blades and put them to numerous uses besides scraping whiskers. There were none for my face growth.

Occasionally a large group of people, including women and children, would visit. The children were naked and many boys and girls were smoking pipes or cigarettes by age eight. Smoking a pipe was an activity heavily indulged in by both men and women.

One of the first natives I had met had black teeth. Later, I noted that many had such teeth. It was later explained to me how they got that way. During peacetime, the people loved to engage in dance and merrymaking. They found that by chewing a certain nut wrapped in a proper leaf and mixed with powdered lime, their spirits were elevated, their joy enhanced, their wisdom doubled, and endless energy was produced. This put greater vigor in their celebrations. The combination, when thoroughly chewed, produced many black teeth.

I began to learn their language. They were eager to teach me. When I produced a sentence, they would laugh and gyrate. I soon learned "kake tulu vate lima vonomo vitu veer zia mano," "va monza sisu, roko sngo," and, "rako sa zoli lalu." They had more fun than I did.

In their society, it was a woman's duty to do routine labor such as growing a garden, cleaning house, raising children, harvesting, and cooking. The man's obligation was to build a house, acquire land, build a boat, fish, and hunt. If there were other people around, the men would negotiate disputes or fight. Fighting, however, rarely occurred.

Their marriage customs had unique features. When love manifested itself and the urge to do something about it became a necessity, the man went to the father of the prospective bride for permission to marry. The father, being responsible for his daughter's welfare for life, investigated the groom's potential for being a good provider. He then granted or refused permission.

If rejected, the suitor had the option to give up or try to prove his worth through some activity. If accepted, the father demanded a payment of money. The money was not the father's to spend, but was kept in reserve should the marriage turn out not to the father's satisfaction. In that case, he retrieved his daughter. He would then use the money for her upkeep.

If the father was satisfied with a prospective son-in-law

who does not have ready cash, he might then demand one or two years of labor. This depended on his judgment of his daughter's worth. The labor might involve building boats or a new house, clearing ground, making tools, or performing various services.

In peacetime, the main industry of these people was production and processing of copra. Periodically, Chinese junks would sail by and trade it for necessities such as cloth, smoke pipes, hatchets, knives, and tools.

Australian planters and American companies like Lever Brothers cultivated large plantations of coconut trees that gave employment and income to the people. On Choisuel, these were scarce. The natives processed wild copra that was quite plentiful.

After a house and land, an item of much value and usefulness was a boat. A boat to them was like an automobile to us.

# Chapter 9

There were two kinds of boats, the dugout and the plank and rib type. The dugout was limited in size by the size of the tree trunk and carried up to six people.

The plank type's size was limited only by skill and the ambition of the builder. They were built up to 30 feet long and three feet wide. They were equipped with prow and stern projections up to eight feet high decorated with carved figures and animal skulls making them look ferocious. They carried up to 15 people.

The planks were hewn by hatchets, on a one-tree, one-plank ratio, to a thickness of about three-fourths inch. Since no nails were used, every groove and hold eyelet had to be preplanned in the hewing process.

When placed on the rib frame, the grooves and eyelets came together in a way that enabled them to be tied together with fibers into a watertight boat. Seams were caulked by tar-like material made from wild plants. Usually, the boat needed 10 to 12 planks about six inches wide. It took up to two years to build, a great opportunity for a son-in-law to be.

Headquarters was not in a hurry to send a rescue ship. So I had fun with the native-people. I enjoyed them and they seemingly enjoyed me.

Having been surprised by Gordon's excellent command of English, I inquired about it. He explained that the islands were under Australian control. Australians promoted literacy and encouraged their people to go to school. Those with qualifications were encouraged to go to high school in Australia and to the university in the Fiji Islands.

Gordon had taken advantage of these opportunities. He had graduated from Fiji University and had been enrolled in medical school when the war broke out. He returned to Choiseul to assist in ousting the invaders.

He took charge of the transceiver stations while the coast watcher was away, and reported daily happenings and observations. He taught English to those who had an interest, and gave medical first aid to downed American airmen.

He sometimes talked in a brooding manner about his ultimate future once the Japanese evacuated, peace came, and he completed medical school. He planned to return to Choiseul and his people. He sometimes questioned the wisdom of returning to a place that had no medical facilities and where he would be educated beyond the demand of native living standards. He was equipped to run where crawling was all that was needed.

We discussed his dilemma at length. The most comforting thing I could tell him was that he would be like a very tall person among short ones. He would see what they see, only much farther. He could also take pleasure in knowing and understanding things that others might wonder about or be fearful of.

Knowledge and understanding are never burdensome and may be considered a kind of a gift. People have a great variety of gifts, but no one has all of them. Some people are able to make beautiful music by instrument or voice, some have athletic skills, some write poetry easily, some have acute insights about human drama, and so on. By his association with these simple folks, he could help them acquire new insights, and thus progress. In general, Gordon agreed to these views.

On the fourth day at the camp, while I sat in the hut contemplating and trying to compose some poetry, an anxious looking fellow appeared from the bush. He reported that, from a river to the west, a Japanese patrol had disembarked and was headed toward our camp.

The natives quickly assembled into a circle with Tomsoy in the center. For a while, silence reigned while he contemplated our intense countenances. Finally he said to me, "There are two things we can do. Set this place on fire and run, or defend it. There are six or eight of them. You, an American Army officer, have a suggestion?"

Instantly, I began to recall my training in the infantry and how the situation could be met. I suggested that we try to defend the location.

Tomsoy discussed with about a dozen natives what was to be done. I anticipated confusion, hesitation, and reluctance. Not at all! Everyone reacted like members of a trained American Army unit. I was surprised. While rifles and grenades were being issued, Tomsoy and I made a plan of deployment.

We were going to ambush. We planned on eight Japs approaching in single file about 10 feet apart or in an 80 foot column. The men were to be deployed six on each side of the most probable approach path. This would cover about 100 feet of the path. I was to man a machine gun located on the opposite side of the building from their approach. I would fire from beneath the structure that was on four-foot stilts.

Tomsoy would situate himself so that he could attack the last man from behind. He quietly talked to his men before they calmly marched off into the bush.

Gordon and I set up our gun. I had used this kind of a

gun before. It was like a stovepipe about 3-1/2 inches in diameter with a barrel through the center. The round ammunition drum rested on top. Outside these dissimilarities, all else seemed to operate like our water-cooled Browning through which I'd fired a million rounds.

We settled down to wait. I was to fire first, which would signal for all to fire like hell. Gordon settled to my left with a rifle. As we waited, my calmness began to evaporate and five minutes later strong nervous shakes began to move up and down my body. It was an enormous struggle to keep control of myself. I felt an urge for action. I wanted to seize the gun and dash down the trail and meet them.

I glanced at Gordon. His face and eyes were stern and motionless as he gazed toward the expected approach. He didn't seem to shake but the grip on his weapon seemed very tight.

I calmed down and thought about what we were doing. I hoped they would come in bunched up. Firing would begin when they were about to reach the building.

Tomsoy and his men would attack from behind. Our plan was to dispatch all without leaving the slightest trace.

A feeling of nausea crept into my being. I helped dump 2,000 pounders on all types of installations populated with people and maybe killed many. We sped away from the scene and saw no blood. Here, for the first time, I was to do the supreme thing eyeball-to-eyeball.

Finally, I thought, "Dammit, they're not down here to shake hands." As we waited, the shakes resumed. Why in hell don't they hurry up and come so we can get it over with. Probably the most agonizing pain for a soldier is waiting for anticipated deadly action.

After an hour, we heard sounds in the bush exactly from

the spot we anticipated. Gordon sighted down his weapon and I through mine. A black face appeared. Japs weren't black. More black faces appeared.

The first one was Tomsoy followed by his dozen. We waited cautiously to see if there were Japs behind using them as a shield. It was a tense and uncertain moment. Fortunately, it did not last long and in a few minutes everyone was talking rapidly and laughing.

Relief was great. Every inch of skin seemed to loosen and flow off my body. We put away the weapons. I wondered if these guys were as relieved as I was. I certainly didn't want to ask them if they'd shaken as they waited.

Tomsoy described what had happened. The six-man Japanese patrol had been decoyed into taking a false trail. These natives were clever beyond description. When constructing this complex, pains were taken to keep approaches to it as wild and undisturbed as possible. They'd even skillfully placed fallen trees as obstacles to discourage march toward our refuge.

A well-beaten trail was made from the riverbank, up and around our camp, to a hill about a quarter mile to the east. There, signs were arranged to give the impression that the natives made fires, danced and frolicked there. It was arranged to look harmless and neutral. From there, the well-beaten trail continued about two miles eastward to a place on a river that flowed northward to the sea. It was known that the Japanese loathed going into the jungle unless forced. If there was an easy way to go, they took it. The complex's location was not compromised.

The natives resumed their normal routines and quietly went about as if the event that just transpired was a common occurrence. I walked around to burn off the tension in my system. We'd avoided a bloody episode and

I felt very lucky.

Euphoria was about to settle in when a realization jarred my inner harmony. This was war. It was expected that every armed person dispatch as many of the opposition as possible. These Japs, who were spared this day, would possibly be back another day to cause mischief.

A feeling of failure to accomplish settled over me like a fog. One of my biggest motivations for surviving was to live long enough to accomplish something. "To leave the world a better place than I found it," as some forgotten poet put it. How would killing a bunch of people make this world a better place? I said to myself, "Hey you! You're a soldier and that's what's expected of you. Victory will make it a better place and victory requires eliminating the opposition. A good world means dead opponents."

It was impossible for me to sleep that night until I pushed a thought button to thoughts of home and the girl I yearned to touch and hold.

What was this strange connection that united hearts half way around the world? It is a connection that fed hope, sustenance, and love to all of us caught in this chaos and madness. Through it came a light that showed there was something around besides hopeless gloom. It made me feel that we were a part of a lot of people. The connection was made very real through letters from loved ones. How we lived and waited for them and read them over and over.

At this time, I felt a longing and a need for a word from her. I thought of my crew at Guadalcanal and hoped they retained all my mail.

Days passed and not a sign of rescue was evident. I felt anger slowly building up.

The natives were very good at keeping me comfortable and entertained. It helped that we liked each other.

Pulsumboie was especially helpful and lovable. Still, my desire to get back to the 307th persisted. "Dammit," I thought, "why don't the bastards hurry up?"

About the third day after the scare Tomsoy said, "Let's go fishing." About ten men filtered into the camp, gathered up a variety of paraphernalia, and in a single file marched out. There were five men ahead of me and five behind. Everything possible was carried on their head or in fiber bags slung over their heads. This left their hands free to swing about or gesture vigorously when talking.

As usual, the march was silent for the first five minutes. We picked our way through the thickness trying to leave no trace of our tracks. We found a worn trail and settled into a military-like march for about three miles. One by one, they settled into songs. Volume and vigor increased as the march continued. The songs they sang were those I recognized from elementary school. They sang them in their own language.

We arrived at the river at probably the same spot the Japs reached a few days before. The men reached into the bush and pulled out three well-hidden canoes. From there, it was about half-a-mile to the Pacific Ocean. After about an hour of vigorous paddling eastward we came to a place where the sea was shallow for a considerable distance from the shore.

Tomsoy said, "We fish here." I wondered how since no one had fishing poles.

From their pouches and bags came dozens of New Zealand hand grenades. They were somewhat bigger than American ones and were dark brown in color. The men said they liked them because they had more power than the American or Japanese ones.

We drifted about until a school of about a million fish appeared. The men stood up and tossed a grenade into the middle of the school. The fish, instead of fleeing, rushed to examine what had been dropped. The grenade exploded and a thousand fish turned belly up.

The natives excitedly jumped into the ocean and gathered the stunned fish tossing them into the boat. One man in each boat stood and watched for sharks. This was exciting to everyone including myself. After the next grenade, I jumped overboard to help in the gathering.

I was surprised at how pleased the natives were to have me participate, and embraced and patted me on the back. I felt like one of them and they accepted me as if I were their own.

The boats were quickly filled. We had to discontinue because we were running out of places to sit. We probably had 500 pounds of fish in the three boats. Close to shore we headed westward.

As we paddled, seemingly by prearrangement, a native appeared out of the jungle with a sack. Laughingly, we'd fill the sack with about 20 pounds of fish and moved on. There were voluminous word exchanges between the givers and the receiver.

This exchange was repeated about a dozen times along the way until there were only two meals worth of fish left by the time we reached our river. It was amazing how generously these guys gave away their harvest.

Going back to our base was the same as coming out, only in reverse. Each of us carried between five to ten pounds of fish.

The evening was spent roasting and eating fish with a great number of guests. Among the guests was a tiny white man. He was introduced as a French missionary priest. He was very talkative, and described his life in some detail. However, his manner and thought process indicated that he had lived in the jungle too long, and was quite out of touch with reality.

His entire life, since ordination, had been spent in the bush. Mostly isolated places. He circulated freely among the Japs as well as the natives. This was frightening considering how freely he talked without much reflection on what he said. The natives were polite to him but didn't take him seriously. They often laughed about him when he was out of earshot.

During our visit, he produced a picture of a human skeleton. He summoned the young natives. Pointing to the picture he said emphatically, "Manuru! Manuru! Manuru!" which meant, a devil, a devil, a devil. Later, these youth mocked him saying, "We know it is a skeleton of a man. He thinks we're dumb." Also, he complained sadly about the lack of holy water during the war.
After the feast, a long visit, and with a full stomach, he departed. He had a mass to conduct.

Daily communications with Tulogi continued. Message exchanges were made as quickly as possible to prevent the Japanese from establishing a fix on our location. Every other day we reminded them of my presence, and they acknowledged saying they would come.

I visited with the people, wrote poetry, sang songs with them when I knew the tune, and brooded.

There was an endless procession of natives coming by, just to shake my hand and express sympathy that I was not with my people. They showed delight in my interest in their things, their language, prayer sessions, songfests, fishing, and manning the machine gun.

They said I was part of them. Once in awhile one would be bold enough to suggest that I live with them. I would tell them there was a girl in America waiting for me. "Oh," they would say, "you can't leave her."

One day, about the 20th of November 1943, a huge,

redheaded, bearded, white man appeared out of the wild. His shirt was unbuttoned and his broad hairy chest stuck out. He came up to a surprised me, stood, and looked.

He recognized my fright, and enjoyed it for a while. This could be a Jap I thought, but he is too big and does not look like one.

On his head was a broad-rimmed hat. At his side an American 45-caliber automatic pistol with lots of ammunition.

I had my pistol in my shoulder holster and I wondered if I could draw it faster than he could.

After savoring my obvious discomfort, he stuck out a large hand and said, "I am Nick, one of two coast watchers on this island. I'm from Australia. I heard you were here, so I came to see you. How are you?"

My heart was beating at maximum RPM by that time. I stuck out my hand and made a good shake. I spoke for some time while he smiled and waited. He knew what he had done. His size alone had an awesome effect, magnified by his sudden appearance, and manner of approach.

The natives came running and offered greetings. This was like a reunion. Exchanges flowed back and forth until the big man put his arm about me and said, "Let's go to the house and sit down and talk." And we talked.

He had me describe what had happened, how we operated as a heavy bomb group, the make-up of our squadron, and such. His particular interest in the characteristics of the B24 made me wonder why he didn't know more about it already.

About the American withdrawal from Sangigai he explained that it was not a defeat as claimed by the Japanese. It was feint to draw attention away from a main operation against Bougainville. It was a success and also took attention away from our suspected location. He and the other coast watchers had assisted in the operation. He said there was more to do. The next morning he disappeared the same way he'd appeared.

November days followed one another like ducklings following mama duck. One day, about the 26th of November (my birthday), a message came from the Naval base at Tulogi to procure a Japanese prisoner.

Tomsoy assembled about ten armed natives and stalked away into the wilds. They were gone two days, which caused Gordon's and Palsumboie's faces to become a little long.

On the morning of November 28, they marched in with one young, skinny, sparsely whiskered Japanese soldier with short crew cut hair.

He and I were exactly the same size. He looked like he had been through an ordeal equally as rough as my own, or maybe worse. He looked undernourished.

The natives had him thoroughly bound with rope. His wrists were tied behind him. Three natives armed with Japanese rifles, marched him at gunpoint to me.

I looked at him and he at me. I could not tell from his expression how he felt. His eyes appeared quite blank. I could tell he did not lead a life of fun, and I truly felt sorry for him.

I wanted to say, "Untie him," until I recalled reports about Japanese treachery, even attacking medics who were trying to save their lives. He was lead away and spoon-fed. They fed him as long as he would eat. He ate a lot.

Tomsoy related how the capture was accomplished. Early in the afternoon, they had encountered a patrol of eight troops. They shadowed it until evening and suppertime. At this time, the Japs had stacked their rifles and bunched up to prepare their meal. It was almost dark when they gathered to receive their cooked ration. They were attacked from all sides. All were shot except one whom was a little separated from the group. He was rushed and bound.

The dead were each dragged to different places and buried. All traces of their presence were hidden. The prisoner was marched to our base for a report. I asked why more than one wasn't taken. The Navy would have appreciated it. "We had orders to capture only one," was the reply. "Orders is orders," is how the saying goes.

Gordon asked if I would come with him to compose a message about the captive. We composed a short message saying that we had the prisoner as requested. We encoded and sent it. We received acknowledgement with instructions on how the prisoner was to be picked up the next morning, November 29.

A seaplane with a B25 escort would arrive at a given point. If it was safe to land, a quick smoky fire was to be lit on the beach. A quick landing would be made, a cargo of supplies unloaded, and the prisoner loaded. Then, there would be a quick takeoff. Nothing was said about picking me up. "They certainly know I'm here," I thought.

The word spread rapidly that a seaplane was coming tomorrow and that I would leave on it. The natives came in great numbers to wish me luck, shake my hand, and say they were sorry to see me go. Most stayed overnight, sleeping on the ground.

Many would approach the Japanese prisoner and in good English shout, "Tojo, eat shit!" If he understood he showed no sign. I felt sorry for him. We probably would have made good buddies in more sane times. Even though the prisoner was carefully guarded by at least three men at all times, I kept my gun ready. Should he escape to tell what he had seen, severe damage would be done.

Next morning, November 29, there was a lot of activity

after the usual prayer ceremony. Over a hundred natives stayed overnight and more kept coming. There was a roar of talk and laughter mixed with expressions of sorrow to see me leave. I worried that with the arrival of so many people they would leave traces making this place easy to find. There wasn't much concern about this at the time. I shook hands, hundreds and hundreds of hands. We embraced and shook hands some more. This was both a happy and a sad occasion. We laughed and cried at the same time. How can it be that on the same planet there were people who love us without restraint, and people who craved to kill us?

Nick, the coast watcher, came out of the jungle. He did it to me again. He said, "I am an Australian, paid for and working for the Japanese. We will now deliver you up. All this ceremony and acclaim was to get you to let your guard down and give out information. Now we have it."

It was a most frightening moment, as paralyzing as being in a falling aircraft. However, thinking that all the native hospitality just could not be faked for that long, I acted extremely cool and looked him straight in the eye. I said, "Come on sir. Cut this comedy and let's get going."

He stood and looked determined to follow through on what he'd just said. A few seconds before I would have lost all composure he said, "Yes, lieutenant. I was only joking. Let's get going. After this never, never in this war tell everything to anybody who does not have the authority to know. I had no business knowing about how you operate, but you told me. Be careful."

It was a hard way to learn a lesson, almost a fatal way. War is, as a general said, hell.

Nick talked things over with the natives who assured him all was ready, and that the scouts had reported that where we were going would be clear of the Japanese.

He headed west, followed by hundreds of people skipping about trying not to leave a path or a track. Upon reaching a trail, all took it and marched to the river to an awaiting flotilla of large canoes.

I was put in the center of the largest canoe. The flotilla, loaded to capacity with hundreds of natives, paddled a mile to the sea. When my boat reached the ocean, a big smoky fire was touched off and a seaplane came skimming in from over the horizon. A B25 appeared high overhead and orbited. The timing was perfect. It showed great navigation and coordination.

Loaded canoes surrounded the seaplane, each loaded with people bringing trinkets to trade. Sailors came out to unload a ton of supplies. They unloaded bags of rice, all sorts of canned food, and medical supplies. There were also boxes of small tools, cigarettes, pipes, tobacco, sweets, and other things dear to the natives.

The Navy men traded for trinkets until saturated. Still, hundreds of outstretched hands offered more to trade.

The prisoner was roughly thrown into the seaplane. Inside, he was roughly received by a couple of armed sailors.

When my long boat pulled alongside to put me aboard, a sailor stepped up and asked, "Who in the hell are you?" Trying to hide my shock, I explained the circumstances and who I was. He consulted with the pilot who said, "Yes, I heard there was an Army flyer here. Let him aboard."

The coast watcher made a roaring sound for all boats to clear the plane. All quickly pulled away, with every person waving goodbye. Thus I departed Choisuel, a place where I'd encountered the most tragic and most happy of times.

*Farewell, farewell Choiseul*
*Who of heavenly folk*
*Who nourished my body*
*Who replenished my faith*
*And warmed my soul*
*And now are sending me again*
*To God's great roaring stage*
*To play in the raging drama*
*And bring back the light to the earth.*
*Thank you, thank you*
*For giving me another opportunity*
*To resume where I had left off*
*To do something for the world*
*That so far I have not.*

For some time into the flight, I fought hard to hold back the tears. Tough looking Navy men were around, and the sight of a battered looking Army warrior in tears would have been out of place.

The prisoner, bound tightly at his wrists and ankles, was placed in a seat and fastened securely to it. An angry looking sailor sat nearby with a weapon on his lap and stared at him. He seemed upset for having to go through so much trouble to come after him. "Just let that son-of-a-bitch make one funny move and I'll put his lights out," he growled. I hoped that there would be no funny moves. Tied as he was, he couldn't make one.

It took the seaplane twice as long as it would a B24 to cover the distance to Tulogi. On the way, we spotted a large formation of Liberators with escorts heading west at high altitude. The sight produced a mild nostalgia.

Most of the planes were shiny aluminum that indicated a new squadron or many replacements. It had been almost six weeks since I had flown with my crew. They probably won't recognize me. Though the natives had fed me well, I hadn't gained an ounce of weight. My bones stuck out all over, and a six-week growth of beard adorned my face.

It seemed strange how my rescue was accomplished. The possession of a Japanese prisoner brought an immediate hustle in the rescue department and a vessel was on the spot next morning. After over a month of waiting, my appearance was an unexpected surprise to the guys who came out.

Anyway, I was thankful for this piece of good fortune. The Navy fellows hustled the prisoner away as if he was a newly discovered gold nugget.

I rode 20 miles to Guadalcanal by speedboat and hitchhiked to the 307th. I walked past the headquarters while a number of fellows watched me with puzzled expressions. I walked past operations and by some guys standing in the doorway. One said, "What the hell is this?" They saw a unshaven, skinny creature with uncombed hair, a dirty non-regulation uniform, nonmilitary shoes, and an Army shoulder pistol.

I went to my tent and walked in. In it were three fellows and four bunks. One bunk appeared to have been unused for a long time. I recognized one of the men as our pilot. He was back and flying again.

They took a few seconds to study this strange and unexpected appearance before they recognized me. With a whoop, they jumped up and we embraced. I fought tears with all my might. Soldiers don't cry.

Neighbors came dashing from all around to welcome me back. It was a happy reunion. The squadron commander was surprised and puzzled. He gave me a brief welcoming speech word and a handshake. He said there was something wrong in the way my rescue had been handled. "I was damn mad once," I said, "for those lost, though nothing could have been done. As for me, I'm here."

Our crew gathered in our tent to talk and review recent events. They had been on a raid. Perhaps, the one I'd seen while in the seaplane. They were visibly tired. Our pilot had had less than two weeks to recover from the trauma. Then, he rejoined the squadron and routine flying.

*He was back again*
*And the crew was flying*
*Engines were roaring*
*Flak still spattered.*
*The skins of the ships*
*The Zeroes still dove*
*Into mad barking 50's*
*They fought to keep faith*
*For those who fell*
*The torch they carried high*
*To light a way*
*To finish the job*
*And fly again home*
*To waiting loved ones*

If there ever was an occasion about which a song could have been written, this was such an occasion. There were no musicians, and time oozed along. Through my thoughts flowed a certain amount of poetry. Often, I scribbled it on some scrap of paper. I would study it. Always, I felt I could have been expressed it better and tossed it aside.

★ ★ ★

The last B24 to land on Koli airstrip on Guadalcanal from the October 25 mission had reported, during debriefing, a man in the water at the location where the bomber had gone down. My copilot immediately remarked, "If there is a survivor from that crew, the chances are ten to one that it's Maleckas. I'll betcha money on that." The rest of the crewmen had agreed.

It was on this belief that the crewmembers were able to prevail over headquarters to keep my personal effects stored in our tent and my bunk unoccupied for two weeks. At the end of that time, all was to be shipped home. Our copilot sent a letter to our pilot in the military hospital in New Zealand about a survivor. He quickly replied with a strong wager that I was the survivor and advised them to retain my belongings.

# Parents Get Word That Son Is Found

Telegraphic word that their son, Lt. Frank Maleckas, has been accounted for was received Sunday morning by Mr. and Mrs. Frank Maleckas of Fern.

The parents had received word Wednesday that Lt. Malecas had been reported missing in the South Pacific.

No details of the case were embodied in the telegram, which said that, when further word was available, the parents would be notified.

*About three weeks atfer the crash on October 25, 1943, this announcement appeared in the Ludington Daily News. A similar telegram was received by my mother and dad. The phrase "accounted for" was so vague about my condition that it increased anxiety.*

# Chapter 10

When I had first joined the crew, the pilot had assigned me as safety officer. He reasoned that since I'd survived a crash I would be more effective in making an impression on the crew about "safety measures."

I seriously discussed things to do to increase survival odds. It followed that they treated survival gear with more care and affection. I myself had carried extra paraphernalia aboard on all flights. Everyone thought all those things I had carried and talked about had helped me survive. As it turned out, in time of need, none was available.

On November 9, exactly two weeks after the crash, the squadron had received word of the name of the survivor who was in native hands on Choiseul. The pilot and the crew remarked, "I knew it. I knew it." They kept my bunk unoccupied, expecting my quick return. When that didn't happen, they still waited patiently until the end of November. Maybe, the Navy had sent me back to the U.S. Just before the deadline to send my things away, I arrived.

Exhausted as they were from flying a mission, we engaged in a small celebration. "Man, but you look ferocious," they remarked. "No wonder the Japs left you alone. You're so skinny that anyone looking at you from the side couldn't see you."

Next day, the whole morning was spent in debriefing. The interrogator was a large man, a former professional wrestler. We went over my whole episode in the finest of detail. He noted things that I considered completely insignificant. It made quite a bulky report when it was finished.

I spent the afternoon taking a physical. All seemed well, except for the dramatic weight loss and a large red patch on one buttock. I had felt a sensation there during the last few days but ignored it. With events pressuring for attention and anticipation over returning, I hadn't taken too much note of the buttock.

The doctor recommended I regain weight before resuming full activity. He described how I should eat. The whole procedure was taking up time and I was becoming anxious and fidgety about reading the mail. I hadn't had a chance to look at it, and there was a sizable stack.

First, I sorted out all the mail from Helen. I read each letter slowly, word for word. I extracted all the meaning and feeling from them. Then, I went back and read between every line. There was so much in them that I needed and wanted. I sat and dreamed, allowing the warmth of her words to seep through my whole being. What had happened and what the future held seemed trivial. What magic, I thought, these sheets full of funny squiggles produced in my soul.

There was also an 8 x 10 photo in a gold frame. She looked wonderful.

The copilot took special note, and vented a string of exclamations. He said, "You came away and simply left her! How could you leave someone like her?"

"Well," I said, pointing at a photo of his girl. "You left her didn't you?"

"I was drafted," he said.

"I was drafted, too," I said.

"But you are 24 years old, while I was only nineteen,"

he said.

"Oh, come on Dumpy," I said. "At that age you run out of excuses. You're just too slow."

"At 24 you're losing speed, too," he replied.

We went on and on for a while. Finally he said, "By golly, I've had enough missions so that I might be able to beat you home. If you don't marry her and have a kid before I do, I'll be mad at you. I plan to have a lot of kids."

"I plan to have some but I won't race with you. You're too much like a rooster," I said.

This probably wasn't so, but I had to top him. He always spoke about his large family and how he liked kids and planned on having a number.

The pilot had nothing complimentary to say about kids.

"Those squally, drippy-nosed brats! I won't have any," he would remark.

"Well," the copilot would quip, "maybe you won't, but your wife may." The bombardier had his own attitude. "Oh hell," he would say, "get drunk, treat your women rough. They like it best that way."

There were a few letters from Mom and Dad. They'd gotten a telegram soon after the crash and had stopped writing. I imagined Dad's stony silence and Ma's constantly flowing tears. I sat down and wrote letters for two days.

On the fifth of December, I flew a mission with my crew, not as a navigator, but as an observer. There was the usual tension and complete lack of fun.

The altitude seemed to cause the redness on my butt to swell and hurt. A few days later, I went up on a check flight in the morning and flew a compass swing in the afternoon.

The pain in my rear could no longer be ignored. The

flight surgeon finally said, "Perhaps we were pushing you to soon. With what you went through, I'm going to recommend 30 days in the hospital. What I see doesn't look good." He did not say what was wrong, and in those times one didn't ask.

Through December, I lingered in a New Zealand hospital while the outbreaks on the buttock became more painful and spread to the back of my neck. I now had a pain in the neck. The red bumps developed into huge carbuncle-looking affairs that didn't respond to any treatment.

For a week they would subside only to flare up again and swell to even larger abscesses. Various doctors looked at them, said something to the attendants, and went on.

With bandages covering the infected places, I sauntered about the hospital. It was December and Christmas time. New Zealanders were putting up nativity scenes, mowing around them, and watering flowers. Flowers were in full bloom everywhere. It was strange to think of this being Christmastime.

Toward the end of December, I was summoned before a committee of doctors who informed me that my condition could be better treated in the United States and that I would be sent there. That's what I'd wished for, but I could not bring myself to be happy over it. It meant giving up my crew for good. It also meant I had not done my full share of work in this campaign. I felt like a leaf tumbling in the wind. I had no control over where I was going.

It took 15 days to cross the Pacific in a converted hospital ship. Before we were out of sight of New Zealand, an Army captain assembled the officer patients aboard and described an extreme military SNAFU on the ship. It dealt with feeding the troops, all of which were patients representing a full spectrum of disability. Hence, none could be made to work unless they volunteered. No provision had been made to put a responsible officer in charge of food services, but the coolers were fully provisioned.

A pleading presentation was made for one of us to volunteer and be responsible for feeding the troops for the duration of the voyage.

There was silence as the officers looked down at the floor. Feeling that I hadn't yet done enough, I agreed to take the responsibility.

I was given a small office, a microphone to communicate with the passengers, and a set of keys to all the food lockers. The Captain said, "The next meal is at eighteen hundred." Then he left. He was very hard to find during the rest of the trip.

Finding volunteers was almost impossible. All of the troops were hard-boiled men. All were hurt or wounded in some way. Now, they were committed to the old military maxim, "Don't volunteer for nothin'."

Most of the troops were Marines who maintained an unfavorable opinion of the Army. Their attitude, "Don't let the Army tell you nothin'."

My call over the speakers yielded no volunteers. I went up and down the deck and confronted the men on a one-to-one basis. The Marines refused, but I found five Army men who agreed to help out "just this once."

These volunteers were inexperienced men in handling food. We managed to put out a meal. It was poor, but we all ate. My volunteers did their job as promised and disappeared in the crowd.

There were about 400 troops aboard. It was a repeat for the next meal, and the next, and the next. The meals were as good as an infantryman or a tank man could produce.

But to the Marines, who as yet had not furnished a man to help, it was unacceptable.

They complained loudly and looked surly when I walked among them. I felt that they would gladly throw me overboard.

"Why don't you help?" I asked.

"We won't until the chow gets better," they replied.

"How can you expect it to get better if you don't help?" I asked.

"The food should get damn better soon," they threatened.

We were only three days out, and there was no authority I could turn to. The captain who assigned me the position was hard to find and knew nothing about feeding large groups.

On the fourth day, God sent me an Army sergeant who in my situation should be called a savior. He was a broad, powerful looking, black-haired Italian with long arms. His voice was a deep bass.

"Lieutenant," he said. "I feel that you're having trouble. There's more coming. I have some friends who will help you. I am from artillery, but have done some cooking. Let me do what I can."

I wanted to embrace this wonderful, rough-looking man. "Sergeant," I said, "I've been killing myself trying to put a cooking crew together. You are a Godsend!"

For the next 11 days he and his five assistants seated themselves over large cook stoves and saved the voyage from ugly events. The Army came through and saved the Marines.

My great regret is that at the end of our voyage I did not thank him, embrace him, obtain his address, or communicate with him.

Somewhere in this country there walks a great, great

Army sergeant who performed a deed more noble than he'll ever know.

On the 15th day, San Francisco appeared on the far eastern horizon. How pleasant it would have been to be coming back with Big Moose and the guys who went out with it. I recalled watching the spinning propellers, and listening affectionately to the hum of the motors. How they had become a part of me. How its destiny and my own became one. Now, this almost human machine was somewhere in the big deep's grave and the crew was no longer together. I felt compassion for their replacement navigator, and hoped nothing would ever happen to him, for he was I. With every bit of good fortune I encountered, there accompanied a feeling it was undeserved.

I spent a month (January 1944) in Letterman General Hospital with no success. They sent me to a hospital in Temple, Texas. I stayed during February. Here they treated soldiers with very serious problems. Patients without legs or arms were predominant here. By the beginning of March, my ailment seemed under control. The staff recommended and I was granted a 30-day sick leave.

During this period I decided to get married if Helen would say yes. I wanted to marry the girl I'd had my eye on since I'd first seen her at age five. Events had prevented us from dating or spending much time together. We dated through correspondence.

I had felt more and more delight as time passed. Now was the opportunity. She was in the morning of life, and I was, perhaps, an hour or so further along. I kept her picture out wherever I'd settle. Friends would comment, "If you don't grab her quickly, you'll be the dumbest guy I ever met." On March 15, on one of the coldest and slipperiest days of spring and after using up all of Dad's rationed gasoline, we had a wedding.

It was a Polish-like affair with Lithuanians, Czechoslovakians, and nearby neighbors attending in large numbers. Piles of homemade sausage and wine made it difficult for these farm folk to go home until sunrise. Only the beckoning of the cows summoned them home. Our honeymoon was a trip across Lake Michigan on a car ferry.

My sick leave orders indicated that I report to Atlantic City at the end of 30 days. This was the Army's way to recognize the troops who were in combat. This gave them a bit of the best the country could offer.

For a week we lived graciously while the old ailment returned and became meaner than ever. Large, red, swollen blotches appeared all over my face and belly.

Doctors hastened me back to Temple, Texas, and further treatment. This time the doctors said, "We can't fool around with this any longer. We've been on this case for five months. We'll use a new medicine, one we use as a last resort." It was penicillin that they were talking about. It was new, scarce, and not very potent. It was used only in emergencies and in very severe cases.

It was administered with a large needle into the buttock every three hours for 30 hours. At the end of the series, the doctors gathered about to observe. It worked well. All growths stopped immediately and disappeared. The ugly scars began to fade. In a week, the medics released me. I received orders to go to Louisiana and military instructors' school.

Here the returned officers were taught how to teach. I felt the teaching methods I was taught were superior to those taught in college. I became a full-fledged army instructor and was ordered to teach at the navigator's school in Hondo, Texas. Hondo was the least desirable place to be stationed.

When I graduated from navigation school in the class of 4213, in October 3, 1942, the Army Air Corps was in a rapid state of expansion. It needed many instructors, and quickly. The top ranking graduates were retrained as instructors. I'd not been in that group and had served with an operational group. I was now returning after my tour. Here in Hondo, I found some of my classmates who were still teaching.

It was good to see them, and we engaged in numerous mini-reunions. One by one as they returned, battle-tested pros released the old instructors for overseas duty. Veterans gradually became our teaching staff.

I seized my new job with fervor. I felt the shortness of my overseas tour had left me with much to do.

I was promoted to captain and navigator student flight commander. Three returning instructors and five original instructors staffed my flight. The pace was rigorous. Expanding B29 forces as well as the older B24 and B17 groups devoured our graduates as fast as we turned them out. The B29 campaign against Japan was beginning and bombing over Germany intensified.

There came a day in December that shocked all of us at Hondo. The Battle of the Bulge exploded and was felt all over the country. Evidently, panic gripped the highest echelons. Orders came to assign all no-prior combat navigators to fighting units and ship them out. It happened that only two instructors and I were left to do the work of eight.

Graduation was about three weeks off. The work pace for those of us left became exhausting. Flight commanders recommended that graduation be postponed. Orders came back that all classes would graduate on schedule, and that we would make do with what we had.

Pilot schools, bombardier schools, gunnery schools, and

aircraft production lines were now coordinated. No sector would hold up the rest. The three of us worked at least 16 hours a day. The classes graduated on schedule. During this period our wives received very little smooching. We were genuinely exhausted. All of the young instructors were married and with difficulty had found places for their wives. During this crisis, some of us felt foiled. However, relief came quickly. A couple of all "A" sharpie graduates and a new bunch of fire-tempered veterans joined the staff and were distributed among the flights. At Hondo once again, the war resumed a normal pace.

I noted a sharp difference in my navigation skills as compared to when I graduated. When I took my students up on a navigation problem, I found it quite simple to find location, wind direction, and speed. As a student it had been a sweaty struggle and I had often made errors. It was fun observing students knowing exactly what they were doing and what the results would be.

Actual operational experience was a big help and students gave a more attentive ear to returnee instructors. I enjoyed teaching and put a great deal of effort into it. Working with very motivated students added to my satisfaction and feelings of success. Also, I had two hard-working instructors who had done a tour with the Eighth Air Force. Their wealth of experience precluded illusions that students might have developed.

Our whole training machine settled into a well-organized routine. Classes graduated and quickly sped off to waiting units as new groups of fit young men refilled classrooms.

Peace came to Europe in May 1945. A new class of about 400 navigators graduated and became second lieutenants. The pipeline that had rapidly siphoned away the graduates when the war was intense stopped. It began to back up.

Even with the war accelerating in the Pacific these hundreds of new combat men temporarily accumulated while new recruits came in. There was a noticeable change in the men's attitudes. The atmosphere of tension, of urgency, and of purpose relaxed. Some began to behave as if the war was already over and their discipline sagged.

We now had a two-fold assignment. We were to train a new class and find useful tasks for the recent graduates. Normally, newly commissioned men shipped out in three or four days. A certain amount of fooling around was accepted while they waited for assignments. Now, the length of inactivity was not definite and they were required to stay on the base during the day. To men who were young and at the peak of energy, this was like putting a hungry goat in a cabbage patch and telling it not to eat. They wanted to go to town, San Antonio, to roar.

Orders came down to keep the men purposefully occupied and on base. How we were to do this was not specifically outlined. It was up to us. We began to dig in and develop a program that we felt was useful and purposeful. It meant extra time researching and preparing. We still had to teach the newly arrived class. We decided to present important topics that had not been heavily stressed during regular training. Topics included uniform regulations, military correspondence, gunnery and ballistics, and military law. With the help of an assistant, I researched, wrote, and researched some more. We perspired a great deal during the heat of the day and worked late. Each of us had a sweet wife waiting somewhere in Hondo swatting away at cockroaches all day long. There was enough war for both men and women at this time.

Near the end of the third week, we were nearly

exhausted. Fortunately, all the new navigators were absorbed into active units, mostly by B29 groups. My assistant, an ambitious Eighth Air Force veteran, and I talked about how we regretted missing the B29s. We admitted that bravery was not our biggest assets, but if a call was made we wouldn't hesitate to quickly accept.

He had flown a full quota of the meanest missions over Germany with the Eight Air Force. We both had seen war to its fullest and had little appetite for another swing. If drafted, we would go. Just like we had in the first place.

Kinship and affection grew strong between us. We were like two hotdogs that went through the same grinder. He came from a Polish family of limited means. I loved his attitude. He gave his fullest measure of devotion and he was always concerned that he didn't do enough. He would often remark, "Come on and lets get to work and get this son-of-a-bitchin' war over with so we can go home." With that, we tore into son-of-a-bitchin' work to get the war over with.

In most of the stories and poetry dealing with war, I recalled terms such as victory, glory, courage, and liberty. After reading them, I perceived war as men charging into a foray shouting, "to victory", "to glory", and "for liberty" while planting a flag somewhere. As it turned out, it was mostly, "Dammit, do I have to do this?" or, "Let's get this over with, I want to go home." Also, much was done in silence, dread, and hope.

July was hot in Hondo, Texas. Numerous battled-tempered veterans gradually filtered into the base. They were in various stages of transition. Some waited to be sent to the Pacific; some waited for orders to the training command; and some waited to be discharged from the service. The Pacific war was in full fury. Students began to realize that the war wasn't over and were again serious about graduation and receiving a commission.

As flight commander, I signed hundreds of diplomas and papers. I kept in touch with my crew in the Admiralty Islands. They were past due for return to the United States.

The copilot had been promoted to full pilot and had a crew of his own with which he was pleased. The original crew had been split up between the two pilots.

One day my letters were returned indicating both pilots were lost along with their crews. Where and how I never learned. A depression hit me and it became quite hard for me to work. I became tired and stayed tired. Maybe I had done enough and had accomplished something. It had been over three years since I'd received my commission. Since that time I had pushed myself beyond my capacity. I began in the Army not knowing what a commission was. Now, I was a Captain. Usually, I was a quiet and a meek guy. I was now bellowing at the troops. In my father's world the son of a muzhik could never become an officer. Still, I was one. I could possibly be sent anywhere in the world. My signature was on over a thousand graduation documents. I'd navigated a B24 across the Pacific and had patrolled over a million square miles of the ocean. I helped to drop hundreds of bombs on the Solomon's. Perhaps I should cease feeling I hadn't done enough.

War in the Pacific was progressing favorably with the capture of Okinawa and Iwo Jima. From high headquarters came the policy that troops who served overseas and had earned sufficient points could apply for release from service. Men by the dozens took advantage of the policy and went home. These were the fellows who had flown a great number of nasty missions over Germany and in the Pacific. They were really fatigued. I began an inner debate with myself about whether I had done my job and should go home. I had accumulated more than enough points.

While debating, I continued to teach and found that I was good at it and liked it. With the war in Europe over the atmosphere and attitudes changed. Troops needed more motivation and the officer staff was assigned to extra duties. Many were quite nebulous in nature.

Troops who were "fight" oriented began to find that duty was becoming less of a challenge. The extreme urgency that had characterized our work routine began to fade.

Finally, I made a decision in July of 1945. I would work with the current class and upon its graduation I would apply for discharge. My military career that began in April 1941, ended in July 1945, after 51 months of service.

# Epilogue

Like Johnny, in an old musical, I came marching home and out of the maelstrom of the past four years. The war was still raging full throttle in the Pacific. It made me feel that I had "bugged out" a bit too soon.

In September the war ended, the guns went silent, the lights came on again all over the world, and I felt better. The air smelled better and the birds sang sweeter. As the odious scoundrels were eliminated, the world at last was made safe for democracy.

I became a science and mathematics teacher in the Frankfort Public Schools. It felt good to be teaching people to create rather than to destroy. However, this time of good feeling was short lived. A predatory ideology began to emerge. It was similar to the one against which we had just spent blood and treasure to subdue. Its proponent, Khrushchev, vowed to "bury you" (us), and promised that our children would grow up in a communist world. This was a big no-no to me.

The term "Cold War" became a part of the lexicon of the day. It produced an ominous atmosphere in our daily lives. Again, the world became a dangerous place. The country began to arm itself.

I began to feel that I must become militarily involved. So, I sought and joined an active Air Force Reserve unit. Now, I practically had two full-time jobs, each very demanding. Fortunately, good health, youth, and my father's philosophy, enabled me to survive and give the "full measure of devotion", to full-time teaching and the military obligation.

After 23 good years of active and reserve military duty, I was allowed to retire at a good rank. I continued to teach in the Mason County Central Schools and upon completing my 35th year, I retired in 1980. Been smelling roses ever since.

★ ★ ★

*We took a stance to thwart the foe*
*From those who fell*
*We took the torch and held it high*
*We kept the faith with those who died*
*We bid them rest in quiet peace*
*While great engines hummed*
*To keep a tranquil world.*

With apologies to John McRae WWI

# A Legacy of War

*For them no more the blazing hearth shall burn,*
*Or busy housewife ply her evening care:*
*No children run to lisp their sire's return,*
*Or climb his knees envied kiss to share.*

– *Thomas Gray*

Additional copies of this book can be obtained by sending $14.95 + $.90 Michigan sales tax, + $3.00 shipping and handling, or a total of $18.85 to:

Mr. Frank Maleckas
1075 North U.S. 31
Scottville, Michigan 49454

Canadian orders are $21.95 + $6.00 shipping and handling.

Organization and volume discounts are available.

*Book production by Bookability, Inc.*
*P.O. Box 843, Elk Rapids, MI 49629*
*(231) 264-5851*